Heal Your Heart:

How to Awaken Your Soul with Self-Forgiveness

Charmayne Kilcup, PhD

Book design by Diana Nuhn.
Written by Charmayne Kilcup.

Disclaimer:
Any identifying characteristics such as name and occupation of client examples have been changed.

Charmayne Kilcup, PhD LLC
Visit my website at **www.charmaynekilcup.com**

Printed in the United States of America
First Printing: November 2018

Published by Tom Bird Retreats, Inc.
Published for: Joyful Heart Press

Paperback ISBN: 978-1-62747-331-6
eBook ISBN: 978-1-62747-333-0

For Robert.

Your unwavering presence and love have helped me touch into Soul.

In the immortal words of the great poetess, LuAnne Sugar: "I am obliterated with gratitude."

I am forever thankful.

Contents

There is something important I want to tell you. . . .

Dear Sweet Soul, you didn't do anything wrong.
In fact, *nothing* you did was wrong.
You are a gorgeous divine human being who experienced
something difficult, painful, possibly even atrocious.
You didn't deserve to go through what you did.
You didn't call it upon yourself, or ask for it—even if you
thought you did.
You never did anything wrong.
I tell you this because I know that part of you believes
you did.
This part of you that believes she is bad, worthless, ugly, or
worse.
This part of you that believes what happened was her fault.
But it wasn't.
She is perfect, as she is, right now.
She is undeserving of the hardships she experienced.
And she is starved for love.
This part of you has kept on loving, in spite of it all.
She asks you now to love her, forgive her, and allow light to
enter into all the dark places that shame once occupied.
It is safe to love her.
It is safe to love you.

Foreword

Walking the path of transformation will shake away all things that are not loving so that we are left only with the truth that we are holy beings. I have found that there are few people who actually walk this path and even fewer who expertly guide others down it.

Dr. Charmayne Kilcup is an expert guide who lovingly and gently shepherds the bravest of the brave down the path of their lives into discovering their holiness. Her new book, *Heal Your Heart: How to Awaken the Soul with Self-forgiveness*, is a significant contribution to this work. Dr. Kilcup offers practical ways we can come into cooperation to accomplish the union within ourselves where peace, joy, and healing live.

I first met Charmayne through my work with Dr. Robert Waterman. We bonded talking about nutrition, but her light shines so bright it is hard to not be drawn to her for all her wonderful gifts. Over the years working together in Robert's Mystery Schools, we have borne witness together to the power of forgiveness. But also, over these last years,

Charmayne has become a treasured professional resource for the large group of chronic illness sufferers with whom I work. Over and over again, I hear the voices of my clients and the joy their voices contain when they come in touch with the authentic and vulnerable place inside that holds the healing through forgiveness. I have come to understand through my own journey of healing that our loving holds the power to forgive our misunderstandings, and this is the healing we all search for when we feel stuck or think we cannot take one more step in life.

It is a rare and wonderful thing to find an authentic healer who understands the path of soul transcendence because she herself is traveling it. In reading this book, it becomes apparent that this path is not complicated but instead somewhat straightforward: just be willing to engage what hurts in you. And most important, all the tools you need to do that are available in unlimited amounts within you right now. Reading the warm and calming words that Charmayne has written, I felt hope building inside of myself. Tears welled up in my eyes, knowing that not only are we never alone but also our hurts can be our guideposts.

Over and over again while reading this book, I appreciated the practicality she presents in each of her chapters. Our own loving has the power to reach into all the places we thought were untouchable, unlovable, and unfixable. And, all the things that are painful in our life become the treasure map to get there.

A few sentences that struck me:

x

The truth is you are living love. Sparkling, vibrant, gentle, always present loving. You are beyond good or bad. You are worthy. And you are loving. Our task is one of remembering who we really are. Uncovering the falsehoods and finding the gold that is underneath. We wade past the murky waters of trauma, heartache, and loss and into the crystal-clear ocean of who you really are.

Charmayne, thank you for this. Thank you for your willingness to share this with the world and thank you for creating a way for us to come to the understanding of who we really are. It is truly a gift you are giving the world to help us understand that our humanness and heartache can help us — if we let it. And for those of you about to embark on the journey into your heart reading this book, your holiness awaits you.

Jessica Flanigan, CN, author of *The Loving Diet*

Introduction

I am amazed every day. Every single day I work with a client, talk to a friend, or have dinner with a family member, I hear about the difficulties and challenges they have experienced. Some are slight, such as receiving criticism for a spelling error on a school paper or being yelled at by a stranger for parking over the line. Others are tougher, such as being cheated on, abused by a parent, or molested in a parking garage. My job is to hear about the hard times and help people through their hurt. You would think that listening to these stories all day long would make me depressed and nihilistic. But the reality is, every single day, I am in awe of all the people in this world who are brave enough to keep on loving, in spite of it all. I see hearts that have been abused, stomped on, and dragged through mud; in every one of those hearts, I see a tender place that still courageously opens to loving. I see hearts that more than anything want to love and be loved. And whatever struggle or trauma may have led you to open this book, I know that love lives on within you, too, even if you can't see it or feel it just yet.

My own healing journey, and subsequent career in helping others heal, has taught me something. When I was in a state of near-paralysis from the pain I felt, I wasn't looking deep enough inside of myself. All I could see was the pain. However, when I looked deeper into both myself and my clients, I saw beautiful souls who were still bravely loving those around them. I saw bruised and battered hearts still beating with love underneath it all. I saw gorgeous humans who loved others and still wanted to give and receive love, despite being kicked around by life. Underneath the pain, the wounds, and the hurt existed hearts that were beating with life, longing to release their love and to allow the love around them to enter.

I realized that love lives on. Even when we have experienced anger, rage, and heartache, we still want to give and receive love. Loving doesn't die. It may get covered up momentarily by hurts and wounds and abuse, but it still lingers beneath the surface. Sometimes we build walls and blocks to loving, but even these are never permanent. One day, when time has passed and healing has occurred, that love will break through our emotional barriers and warm everything in its presence. Like a dirty light bulb after being cleaned, love effortlessly and proudly shines through the scars in our hearts. Love is the root of who we are. It cannot be buried or destroyed. Ultimately, love is bigger than pain.

This feeling we call "love" is fierce and strong. Love is like water — silent, quiet, crystal clear -- and powerful enough to carve through boulders. Despite abuse, criticism, neglect, betrayal, and abandonment, our love is like a river — we are unable to keep it contained for long. It will make its way through even the most treacherous of landscapes. Love is as powerful and gentle as the glorious ocean. It is big, deep, and always present, even if we can't see it.

My Spiritual Awakening

From all that I have learned both professionally and personally, I now know that love is the one energy that never disappears. I want to share my story with you so you know who I am, what I've been through personally, and why I teach this work and have written this book. You'll see that I am no stranger to emotional issues, heartache, or spiritual crises. Though my story might seem odd, or even unbelievable at times, I promise you it isn't. I also promise you that you don't have to experience a spiritual emergency the way that I did to acquire the healing you need. My awakening helped me step into a deeper loving, but the techniques I learned as a result of going through a major crisis and coming out the other end will help do the same for you, in a much easier and gentler way.

For the vast majority of my life, I have felt like an outsider. Even as a young girl, I knew my interests were different from my peers' interests. I thought a lot about God. My favorite moments in elementary school were actually when the girls in my class would have verbal arguments and our teacher would send us outside to work them out. I loved sitting in a circle with the girls in my fourth-grade class, talking about our emotions and how we felt and why we were hurt. I loved facilitating understanding between the wounded parties and finding ways we could develop compassion for each other. I wanted to engage in this process more than I wanted to play at recess, read, create art, or even eat lunch. Needless to say, I was a weird kid.

Besides exploring deep-seated emotional issues with my fourth-grade peers, I was interested in spirituality. I remember being eleven or twelve at summer camp and gazing into the stars, with a deep yearning to know and feel God. My best friend and I spent all our time together talking about boys we thought were cute—and the nature of God. These were not normal conversations for eleven-year-olds, but we found both subjects absolutely fascinating (and still do). My quest to understand the universe, and deep existential questions of why we are here, led me to study various religions and metaphysical ideas. In high school, while studying trigonometry, English, Spanish, and chemistry, I read books about astrology and world religions for fun. Though I might have looked like any normal sixteen-year-old, I was interested in ideas and concepts that others didn't and was called "crazy" and "weird" countless times.

As I grew up, my studies in spirituality and psychology continued. Strangely enough, my own spirituality began to deepen when I got really sick. At the age of 23, I found I was overcome with a deep fatigue. It was a tiredness so intense that I could barely function on a day-to-day level. I had weird symptoms such as heaviness in my limbs, nerve pain, nausea, and jitteriness in my body. I would sleep fourteen hours and still wake up exhausted. After nearly losing my job because of my inability to perform at work, I finally went to the doctor and was diagnosed with chronic fatigue syndrome.

The diagnosis brought some mental relief, yet not much else. I knew I was sick, and deep down, I knew it was more than low adrenal function and the Epstein Barr virus the doctors had discovered. So, I decided to really explore it. I intuitively knew something was going on with me. I felt an inner impulse to be still, meditate, and go inward. Truthfully, all I could do was be still and go deep into my inner world and thoughts. Through lots of sitting and staring into space and journaling, I connected with my deepest passions. I realized I felt most alive and vibrant when I was helping people with their daily problems and unresolved issues from their past. I felt the most "juice" when my friends would call me and we could talk about and heal their relationship issues, job issues, or existential crises. In a strange way, the chronic fatigue slowed me down so I could really begin to see who I was and what I wanted. It was in this time of rest that I realized I wanted to be a therapist.

And so, I enrolled at Southwestern College, in Santa Fe, New Mexico, to study Counseling Psychology. I had no idea what I was getting into. It was there that my whole world was blown open. Unbeknownst to me, Southwestern College was the closest place to a real live Hogwarts. It was a school of magic, and it cracked open my brain and my spirit in ways I never could have imagined. I read books on psychology, spirituality, and history that absolutely boggled my mind. For the first time in my life, I couldn't wait to get to class each day, and I was sad when class ended. Everything in me wanted to sit in front of these amazing teachers and learn about concepts and ideas that are largely ignored in our popular culture. I felt as if my spirit were ablaze with passion. Interestingly, my chronic fatigue began to heal. I began to have more energy.

During my second year of studies, I had an experience that changed my life forever. I was feeling particularly burned out with school, work, and adjusting to living with a new roommate. Needing some space, I drove to our family cabin in the woods in Colorado. It was an impulsive move fueled by stress and an inner need to get away. I didn't bring anything with me but my dog and a small bag of clothes. No books, no music, no CDs -- nothing.

I drove the four-hour trip, listening to the radio. When I arrived at the cabin, it was dark. I went inside, fed my dog Ruby, and made some dinner. After dinner, I sat on the couch, wondering what to do. Since there was no TV, internet, or homework to do, I decided I would simply meditate in an effort to entertain myself and relax.

I sat there cross-legged on the brown velvety couch and placed my hands on my belly, the way I had been taught by our family's meditation teacher. I sat there quietly and meditated. I moved my energy downward toward my lower belly and simply felt my body. I had performed this meditation a hundred or more times before, and yet something felt different this time, sitting alone at the cabin.

Suddenly, I heard a voice that felt so loving and comforting. It was a voice that was both inside my own head and outside of it.

It said, "Hello."

I was in such a deep state of peace that the presence of the voice didn't startle me. It surprised me, but I was so relaxed I couldn't bring myself to be alarmed, nor did I sense I needed to be (which was a true departure from my normal, anxiety-ridden self). The voice was gentle, comforting, and wise. So naturally I began a dialogue with it.

I responded with a gentle, "Hi."

The voice then proceeded to communicate with me. It told me about who I was and what I was here to do. It shared with me that, as humans, our work is to get in touch with our deepest loving. We are here to wake up to who we really are — immortal beings who are pure love. Our truest self is the Soul. Awakening is about moving from knowing ourselves as simply human to knowing ourselves as divine expressions of loving. The gentle voice shared with me that each human is part of something much bigger and that it is almost crazy that we could ever feel alone, because we are always connected to our Soul. Our Soul is pure loving, wisdom, and compassion. The Soul has a higher perspective on all the events we encounter as humans and it knows that, really, there is nothing to fear.

The loving voice talked for a while longer and I felt so much warm, comforting energy surrounding me. I felt complete safety and peace. It was wonderful. After a while, the voice stopped communicating. I began to feel aware of the living room as I came back to my surroundings. I felt my body heavy on the couch and took a few deep breaths.

I opened my eyes and looked around. And right away, my brain kicked in and said, "WHAT WAS THAT??!!"

As I returned to a normal waking state of consciousness, the part of my mind that was constantly chattering went a little crazy, as it tried to process the voice I had heard and what it all meant. My mind simply couldn't make sense of the experience. Here I was, a twenty-four-year-old girl with brown hair who watched *Sex and the City* in her spare time and went to the country-western bar on Saturday nights for margaritas and dancing. And then, quite spontaneously, I was conversing with my *Soul.* I had never felt my Soul before; my brain had never felt my Soul. And it simply couldn't make sense of that foreign-feeling energy.

Up to that point, I had known myself and felt myself in a certain way. My name was Charmayne, I was 5'8", I thought a lot about things, and I enjoyed spirituality and my friends. I was from New Mexico, I was a student, and I was a little too focused on dating — I was this very human person. But then this person had an experience that felt as if it reached beyond the body and mind. I felt a presence that was far bigger and greater than anything I had ever encountered. And in that moment, I realized I wasn't just a young woman with a penchant for iced coffee and tattooed men. I was something far bigger.

I woke up the next morning, and immediately upon opening my eyes, I remembered what had happened the night before. And again, my brain started going 100-miles-a-minute trying to make sense of it. At this point, I decided it would be best to get home as soon as possible and be with people again. I started to feel real fear. My brain simply could not process the experience I had, and as it worked faster and faster, I had this feeling I was going to leave my body. It felt as though I might just float away.

I immediately got out of bed, gathered my things, cleaned up, and hopped in the car with Ruby. We headed to my parent's house because I knew I shouldn't be alone. Once there, I told them what had happened and we agreed I needed to see our family meditation teacher as soon as possible to help me understand what was going on.

The next day, I saw Lee Lyon, our family meditation teacher with whom I had worked since the age of 16. He was the only person I could think of who might have a slight understanding of what had occurred and might know what to do. We meditated and he helped pull me back into my body again. I left there feeling I would survive whatever was changing within me. And yet, my brain hadn't slowed down at all. It was still racing, trying to make sense of it. I felt as though I had only a slight tether to Earth. I sensed a cord above my belly button keeping me attached to my own body, but the cord was quite thin. In the days that followed, I did everything I possibly could to ground myself, including sitting on the earth, eating meat, drinking tea, and watching stupid TV. I did anything I could do to feel like that simple twenty-four-year-old girl I had been only days before. I wanted to go back to being that person. Whatever was happening scared me deeply, and I just wanted to feel like my normal self again.

After my session with our meditation teacher, I went home and began Googling "spiritual awakening." Intuitively, I had a sense of what was happening to me, even if my logical mind didn't. I found websites that somewhat described and validated what I was experiencing.

Something inside of me had awakened.

Learning the Power of Forgiveness Statements

About a week after my spiritual emergency, I began a new quarter at school. I knew there was an incredible teacher at Southwestern College that everyone talked about; his name was Dr. Robert Waterman. He was the founder of the college and a legend in the community. I knew of him, but that was about it. A few days after my experience at the cabin, I had my first class with him; I had signed up for it two months earlier.

Carrying an iced tea, I walked into the adobe classroom with Native American rugs on the wall and sat down on one of the eight folding chairs laid out in a circle. I had adopted a technique of always having something to drink, because I knew that if I felt like I was leaving my body, I could take a drink and feel myself swallow. The act of swallowing helped me feel that I was still there, in my body, ingesting tea. So, I held onto that tea for dear life, and every few minutes, I would take a small sip. In between sips of tea, I reminded myself to keep breathing. I knew that if I felt my breath, it must also must mean I was here, alive, in my body. Breathe and sip. Breathe and sip. These were my survival techniques.

A few classmates trickled in. And then Robert appeared. In came this 6'4" monster of a man whose presence immediately commanded respect and attention. He was incredibly tall and stocky, with thick white hair and thick dark-rimmed glasses. He sat down next to me. I had never met him before in my life. And yet, he just looked at me. And looked. And then looked some more.

He said, "Hmmm . . ."

"Yes?" I asked this strange man.

"You're about to leave your body," he said.

"I know! I know!" I replied. I was so relieved to have someone see what was going on inside me that I nearly shouted with excitement.

"Do you want to?"

"No! No! No!" I yelled.

And with that Robert broke out into a wide smile and began laughing hard. He looked genuinely delighted by my predicament. I looked at him completely baffled that he had been able to see what I felt was going on with me but couldn't communicate, much less express to other people. I was relieved and mystified that he understood what was happening and his response was genuine laughter.

In that moment, I knew I was going to be fine. Here was this man who had appeared to see exactly what I was experiencing, even though he had never met me. Even though I was worried I might actually be dying, he looked at me and his response wasn't panic, or alarm, but kind, deep belly laughter. If he wasn't worried about it, I knew I didn't need to be, either.

I felt a tremendous relief. I still felt like I might leave my body, but I wasn't as panicked about it as before.

And with that, Robert started class. He asked each of us to share about ourselves and what we were currently experiencing in our lives. A young man next to me introduced himself and began talking about how he was struggling with trying to quit smoking. Robert looked at him and told him to repeat the sentence "I forgive myself for judging myself for believing I could have saved my dog's life." I sat there thinking, "What? What the hell is going on here? This man is talking about trying to quit smoking, not about his dog. How do we even know he had a dog?" Dutifully, the man closed his eyes and repeated the sentence. His face reddened, he gulped, and two tears leaked out of his eyes. The room was quiet. Eventually, the man said, "I didn't know I felt that way. I didn't know I was still carrying that."

You could have heard a pin drop in that room. *What was happening?* I wasn't sure what to think.

A middle-aged woman, Elaine, raised her hand and volunteered to speak. She said she noticed that her body was craving rest, but she didn't feel she was able to stop moving. She said she pushed herself extremely hard to be successful, to be perfect, and to be the most compassionate person she could be. This time, Robert stared a little past her right shoulder as she spoke. When she finished, he told her to repeat the statement, "I forgive myself for judging myself for believing I've failed my parents." The woman tried to hold back sobs. She then explained that she came from a long line of lawyers and that her family had expected she would become one, too. Her parents were disappointed when she chose to get married, raise a family, and then go back to school to be a therapist. Ever since she had decided not to be a lawyer, Elaine had pushed herself in all her endeavors to try to prove to her parents she was still worthy. Somewhere deep inside, she had formed a belief that she had failed her parents, and she spent the rest of her life working hard to show them she worked as hard as they did—and was worthy of their love.

Elaine cried softly for a few minutes. We tried to avert our eyes and give her some space to release the emotion. Robert's eyes remained glued on her. Finally, she looked up.

Her face appeared soft and content. She looked fifteen years younger and she had a quiet smile on her face. "Thank you," was all she said.

Again, I sat stupefied. How had this stranger been able to walk into a room and pinpoint exactly what was going on with me, and with my fellow students, without even talking to us first? How had this professor been able to find the heart of an emotional issue and help his students release it in a matter of minutes? In my training, we were taught that it could take weeks, months, even years, for a client to work through a psychological issue and that, even then, there was no guarantee it would clear. As therapists, we were being taught how to talk about emotional issues, help clients acquire some self-awareness around them, and, if we were really lucky, help clients eventually release them once and for all. In a matter of minutes, I watched this man, Robert Waterman, use self-forgiveness statements to clear lifelong issues of guilt and shame nearly instantly.

It was almost unbelievable.

Sitting in that classroom (and being somewhat of a skeptic), I wanted to see if what my fellow classmates were experiencing was actually real. I raised my hand.

Robert looked at me with his exacting blue eyes, and I began to talk nervously. "Hi. I'm Charmayne, I'm twenty-four, and I'm originally from Albuquerque. I'm here because I really want to deepen into my own spirituality and connect better to God, or whatever that thing up there is called…"

Robert stopped me. As he had done with the others, he told me to repeat after him.

I said, "I forgive myself for judging myself for believing I am unlovable." Time seemed to stop for a moment. As I repeated the words, I felt something deep inside of me give way. I had just met this man and he knew nothing about me. And yet, he nailed a feeling I had carried my entire life and hadn't even known I was carrying.

Something about the phrase "I forgive myself for judging myself for believing . . ." had a transformative effect. By repeating that exact phrase, it was as if I unlocked the mound of grey tension inside of me and found a secret code to lightness and joy. The core of my being seemed to soften and melt, a pink and golden glow warmed my entire body, and I felt a gentle involuntary smile spread across my face. Images of sadness and rejection had flashed quickly through my mind — as if every moment I had ever felt unlovable flashed into my mind and then out of it completely. I felt a peace I had never known before. I had spent three years in therapy, read countless self-help books, studied astrology, metaphysics, and world religions, and I still hadn't known that I carried a belief that I was fundamentally unlovable. By repeating my belief with the secret formula of "I forgive myself for judging myself for believing . . ." I had released the yoke of self-judgment I had been carrying and unleashed a reservoir of inner peace. It felt as though twenty-four years of rejection, stress, and self-judgment drifted away with one sentence, and the tension I had been carrying in my body all this time simply dissolved.

Twenty-four years of grey unease melted off me in that instant. I felt golden joy arise in my belly for what felt like the first time. I had the sense of wanting to giggle and run around and hug every single person in that room. I wanted to walk outside and play on the lawn and feel the spiky grass underneath my bare feet. My normally anxious mind felt uninhibited and free. I felt like I did when I was six years old and would flood our sandbox with water and play for hours on end in the mud and sand in total all-consuming bliss. In short, I felt alive again.

We continued around the circle in this way until everyone had shared. Some people responded to the work with tears, some with laughter. However, we all experienced a release that day. A few of us even felt a deep and profound peace.

I walked out of that three-hour class mesmerized and giddy. I knew I had stumbled upon something magical. This imposing figure, Robert Waterman, obviously had a gift for identifying beliefs. However, deep inside, I knew that anyone could find these beliefs and use these forgiveness techniques. I felt as though I had tripped over a treasure chest spilling out rubies, emeralds, and diamonds. I knew that the self-forgiveness technique Robert had demonstrated was worth more than gold. It had the power to unlock what we all desperately want more than anything: happiness.

It was after that class that I began to study earnestly with Dr. Robert Waterman. We had a ten-week class with him as part of our required curriculum, and I started looking forward to next week's class session at the very end of each one. I couldn't get enough. He taught us about chanting, words for God, but more than anything, he taught us about self-forgiveness. He seemed to be the only person I could find who understood what I was experiencing. I knew he had some pretty profound abilities, and I knew he was going to help me.

With Robert's guidance, I began to really heal. He had the uncanny ability to see the root of a person's issue and then help him or her dissolve it. It was in that class that I learned a powerful process that completely shifted my life. It helped calm my spiritual emergency and helped me to feel like myself again.

It was this process that changed my life and brought me into greater healing. It has reconnected me with the highest and deepest parts of myself — the loving of my Soul — gently, gracefully, and easily. It enabled me to ground myself, when I thought my world was falling apart. Robert's teachings helped me to understand my Soul and recognize that it is pure loving, which is the heart of all our souls. And that this spiritual awakening I seemed to be having was a call to understand and embrace the loving that was always deeply in my soul but had not yet been felt by my ego.

Slowly but surely, I began to return to myself. I started to feel more grounded. I stopped having to sip tea every few minutes to feel alive. I began to have profound experiences of loving. I felt the cosmic consciousness that holds us all. Even when we feel like we are falling apart, it is still there. I fell in love with Spirit, I fell in love with myself, and I fell in love with this work.

I was so intrigued and curious about the work Robert was doing with us in class that I wanted to study more. His work completely changed my life and helped me integrate my spiritual emergency more naturally into my life. More than anything, his work unleashed the real "Me" inside of me. For the first time, I felt that I no longer had to be *normal* to be loved. I could just be love and be loved, and that was good enough. I realized that my worth wasn't dependent on how beautiful, skinny, or hard-working I was. I was worthy because I *existed.* And that the loving in my heart was enough to make me a good student, a good therapist, a good daughter, and a good sister. My loving was enough. I didn't need to do anything to be worthy; I just had to trust that my loving was enough. I learned all of this through the self-forgiveness techniques that Robert taught us.

I studied with Robert intensely for a year, and I learned several techniques that were so powerful I couldn't stop sharing them with family and friends. I was so in love with this healing work he was teaching us that I looked forward to friends calling me with their problems so I could show them the incredible self-forgiveness technique that had transformed my life.

It was so easy. And so effective.

I knew that what Robert was teaching us was the missing link in today's models of therapy and healing. I knew that what he was teaching went beyond what we were doing in that room, and into the very heart of God itself. I knew that what he taught us would help us heal not only ourselves but also the generations before and after.

Robert taught me invaluable information in his private classes. I learned that after a person experiences a difficult or traumatic life event, she will almost always form a negative belief about themselves or that event, especially if they are young. I learned that these negative beliefs form energy blocks in the body that can lead to feelings of anxiety, depression, internal stress, general tension, and imbalances in the physical body. When those blocks are released, energy and life force can flow again. Once energy starts to flow, we begin to feel a relaxed lightness; a sense of joy and happiness naturally emerges.

I couldn't believe I had never been taught this before. How was this not required curriculum? I felt as though I were finally learning the secrets to true healing. In my extensive course of psychological studies (a BA, MA, and PhD in psychology), I was searching for a tool that could really help people. Intuitively, I felt as though psychology was missing something. I had personally benefitted from therapy and knew it could be useful, but deep down I knew there had to be a way of healing toxic patterns from the very core. Now I knew that to really heal all you needed was a well-placed self-forgiveness statement and a deep breath. You didn't need years of therapy and mental analyzing of how you were parented; you also didn't need special ceremonies or intensive spiritual programs. You only needed to find out how you judged yourself and forgive yourself for it.

Heart & Soul Coaching

Psychology helped me understand why people did the things they did, but what I really cared about was helping people *feel* better. I knew it was one thing to gain insight and self-awareness around an issue, but another to clear the issue from the body and energy field. After my training with Robert, I knew this was the work I wanted to do. When I discovered self-forgiveness, I believed that I had finally found the missing ingredient in true healing. I wanted to help people have these absolutely life-changing moments. I wanted to show them that healing didn't have to be long, painful, or laborious. Healing could happen in twenty seconds. Healing was simply a matter of releasing the judgments we've placed on ourselves and allowing loving to come back and fill us up. It was so easy.

After a year of studying with Robert Waterman, I began experimenting with self-forgiveness in a more public arena, working with people, using these techniques. I trained in Noetic Field Therapy and started seeing private clients. I felt so enthusiastic about the work and still do. It is my passion to teach this work and help facilitate the kind of healing Robert facilitated for me.

Since then, I have studied various healing modalities and completed my MA as well as a PhD in transpersonal psychology. And yet, the most powerful modality I have ever discovered was the simple self-forgiveness techniques that Robert taught me at the age of twenty-four. These are the techniques that I use daily with clients and with myself. I am extremely grateful I was taught these techniques and that Robert has put them out into the world for us all to use. I have seen lives transform and decades of hurt melt away in a matter of seconds.

When I first began to see clients, I would open up their energy field the way Robert taught me to do and start feeling the air around their bodies with my hands. It was incredible. While it looked from the outside like I was only waving my hands six inches above the client, I was actually seeing and feeling a myriad of false beliefs stuck in the client's energy field. I could actually feel — with the palms of my hands — where a client had stuck or congested energies that resulted from false beliefs. False beliefs felt prickly on my hand. Stuck energy felt grey and hazy. Sometimes impressions would form in my mind about the belief. I could see where many women had unresolved issues with ex-lovers, which often felt like sticky tar over their bellies. I could feel where some men were afraid to be their true selves, vulnerable and all, which often felt like hot anger buried in the pelvis. I was able to see where people judged their bodies for not looking "right" or performing the way they had hoped they would. Myriad bits of information presented itself to me, just by "listening" to a client's energy field.

I wanted to help people clear these stuck energies. Occasionally, I could intuitively see what negative belief they were holding onto. Other times, I simply had to ask them about their lives and the belief would present itself. We would then clear it, using the specific belief forgiveness statement that Robert had taught me. I would ask them to say the belief statement aloud and then take a deep breath. I could feel the negative belief and the stuck energy around it begin to dissolve, lift, and then ultimately release. I watched my clients on the table during this process and they would naturally start breathing deeper. Some would cry, some would start laughing, but all would soften. It felt as though a soft light entered each client's energy field and body.

Each and every time, I could feel the entire room shift. It was as if the hard edges released into the softness of a clear, warm ocean. People reported feeling their bodies for the first time, or feeling love for people with whom they had been angry. A sweet lightness would envelop the room and we would both drop deeper into a sense of gentle loving. It felt like the whole room was lifted into the heart of the Universe itself.

The results amazed me. After one hour of work together, people reported feeling lighter, freer, and happier. Their faces looked soft and relaxed. Many people felt as though their lives had changed as a result of one session. And indeed, many people's lives did change. By undoing the blocks in their body and energy system, some people found they were able to pursue their passion and find their purpose. Others began to enjoy their lives and relationships more deeply. People started to appreciate themselves, and as a result, their loved ones.

I had one client who struggled with body image and self-esteem who finally got off the roller coaster of yo-yo dieting and began to feed her body what it actually wanted. Another client quit his degrading job to pursue his love of art and writing. One of my clients had struggled with her relationship with her sister for twenty-two years. After our session together, her anger and resentment disappeared and she was able to interact with her sister in a peaceful and loving way. What I found interesting was that none of these clients made these changes because they felt like they "should" or "ought to." As their energy field began to flow, they naturally wanted to make these changes. There was no willpower or discipline needed. Their limiting beliefs had sabotaged any efforts they had previously made to change. Once those beliefs were forgiven, there was no more resistance. Life became effortless.

Since those initial sessions, my work has expanded considerably. I've taken the techniques I've learned from Robert and decades of spiritual studies and modified them to work both in-person and via long distance. In the first aura balancing I ever did, I opened up a client's aura and was immediately struck by the presence of a spirit guide called Ellavivian. When I relayed this to the client on the massage table, she said, "Oh yes, I called her in to help before we began." It was in this first aura balancing that long latent intuitive gifts began to open up for me. Though I often had premonitions and precognitive dreams as a young child, those abilities largely disappeared as I immersed myself in the task of being "normal." When I began to do energy work, those gifts re-surfaced, which has been immensely helpful in the work I do.

When I work with clients — either in-person or by phone — I am able to sense their energies and the major dysfunctional patterns holding them back. I might receive information about troublesome relationships or deceased relatives who have been trying unsuccessfully to get my client's attention. Sometimes, I see past lives or previous existences that need a little help clearing. What I've noticed is that I'm shown only what is relevant to a client's healing needs at that time. My intuitive abilities come in service to healing, not to explore psychic phenomenon. For this reason, I have always been reluctant to call myself "intuitive" or "psychic." I don't have any interest in proving skeptics wrong or trying to predict the future. In fact, the more I do this work, the more I realize that by transforming everything in our lives into loving, there is no need to predict the future. If we are trying to predict the future, what we are really doing is trying to gain control by knowing what is going to happen so we can be safe. However, when we are in loving connection with our own selves and our Soul, we are already safe.

I have learned and am continuing to learn that the more spiritual we become, the more spirituality becomes about simply being present, enjoying life, and experiencing the deep universal loving that courses through each moment. There is nothing we need to search for, achieve, or aspire to in order to be worthy and living in love. Worthiness and loving are inherent to who we are, therefore there is nothing we must seek. The processes I'm about to teach you are the processes I use to help uncover all the false ways we've decided we are unworthy or unlovable. When we clear those beliefs, we can rest in life and enjoy the first taste of a cup of coffee, the colors of the sunset at dusk, the sound of a babbling brook, and the touch of a loved one's hand. When we get out of the muck of false beliefs, we free our energy so that we can actually savor life. We can deepen into the loving that always exists deep in our hearts and being. And that's when living gets really, really good.

You don't need to be psychic or intuitive to do this work. Those abilities have helped me find client's unconscious patterns quickly and easily so we can clear them. But they are not necessary to find your own.

Why I Wrote this Book

I wrote this book because every day I see hearts that are twisted up with pain, abuse, rejection, betrayal, and abandonment. I see hearts that so desperately want to untangle themselves and feel free again. Few of us are ever taught how to release the knots and wounds in our own hearts. Sometimes we carry them forever. The only tragedy to me is that we live in a culture that doesn't teach us how to heal our own heart wounds. I wrote this book because I want you to have the keys you need to untangle the knots in and around your heart that are causing the stuck energy that holds you back from happiness. Healing doesn't have to be hard or complicated. With a few simple tools, we can begin to uncover the light and joy that is yearning to pour forth from your heart again. You can return to your original state of loving and grace -- and you'll take wisdom and experience with you. This book will teach you the tools you need to tend to that beautiful heart of yours. We will clear up any major events from your history that may be causing you pain or suffering right now. You'll then be able to take these techniques with you as you walk through life and encounter difficult situations.

I am going to teach you the profound techniques I use with my clients to release the false beliefs that limit your full experience of loving. While engaging with this material, if you ever feel unsettled, distraught, or like you want more support, please contact a professional. These techniques are gentle and easy and safe. However, if you feel you need someone to help you with this process, please do not hesitate to contact a therapist, Noetic Field Therapist, or trusted healer. Sometimes we all need support on this journey of healing. I, for one, have worked with several therapists, healers, and meditation teachers in my own journey. If you need help finding someone to work with, I've included a list of resources in the back of this book.

This book is about honoring that big heart of yours that so deeply loves. It is about acknowledging the very real pain that has been part of your life experience. And, it is also about showing you how to wipe away the dirt and smudges that cover your own heart so that loving can shine through clearly again. This book is about finding your way back to the loving that you might feel you lost along the way. It is about digging past the abuses, hurts, and wounds, and unearthing the love again, where it can dissolve all of the pain that once kept it buried.

What I want for you is a heart that feels safe enough to love itself. I want you to be bathed in a warm glow of love that cannot ever be taken away from you or destroyed. Loving is where you came from and it is where you shall return. Tapping into the core truth of who you are — the pure loving that is in your heart — is the secret to making this life worth living.

This book will help you find freedom again. It may be a freedom you experienced as a small child, full of wonder, playfulness, and awe. It may be a freedom you have never known. If you've never felt those positive experiences of joy, happiness, and wild uninhibited freedom, that's okay. You may get to have them for the first time and experience them with all the wonder and openness of a child.

This book will help you find your loving again. It may have been covered up, temporarily blocked by false beliefs, or maybe even abandoned, but it was never destroyed. That loving is still right there inside you, waiting for you. It is like a small puppy, ready to play, lick your face, and warm you up with love. The warm glow of your own loving is waiting to gently bring you back to life, to infuse your life with richness and color, and to make it safe to rest in your heart.

Know that you are one of the brave ones. By starting this journey to untangle your heart, you are changing your life. And in doing so, you are going to be carrying light in the very cells of your body. By uncovering the loving that may be trapped in your heart, you will become a beacon of love for others. You will change lives simply by being the love that is your true nature. Thank you for being willing to heal. Your healing will change the world.

Just a note: You may find yourself resisting reading this book at times. It is never fun to look at the places where we are hurt and wounded. However, I would encourage you to stick with the book and the exercises I've laid out for you. It might feel uncomfortable at first to dive into areas that are achy or dark. You've probably entered into those spaces before, and it hasn't felt very good. But we're doing something different this time. We are looking at those painful places, and we are bringing light to them. This may be a completely new experience for you. We are not going into old wounds to simply re-hash them. We are going in to bring love to them, so they can finally heal.

Finally, I use the word "God" in this book because that is the word that resonates with me. If there is a better word for you that describes the Divine, please use that. Many of my clients have been wounded by their religious upbringings and prefer to use the words "Universe," "Higher Power," or "Higher Self." Use whatever word resonates most in your body and replace the word "God" with whatever fits for you. There is nothing wrong with making this word work for you and, indeed, I encourage you to find what feels right for you.

Onward, we walk . . . into love.

Chapter 1
You Didn't Do Anything Wrong

As you begin your own healing journey, the first — and most important — truth I want you to know is that *you didn't do anything wrong*. Not ever. No matter what you believe about yourself or what happened to you, you didn't do anything wrong. Ever.

You came into this world a blessed wonder child and then life got in the way and covered up your joy, happiness, and loving when you felt your first moments of heartache. Maybe your parents neglected you because of their own exhaustion or ignorance. Maybe you felt rejected or excluded from your peer group or heartbreak at the hands of a boyfriend or girlfriend. We often blame ourselves for these life events and somehow manage to make them our responsibility. Our pain, suffering, and heartache become a way to judge ourselves and make ourselves *wrong*. We use life's events against ourselves. This is human and normal but it isn't the truth of who we are.

1

During that crazy meditation in the mountains, I saw clearly that at the core of every single person there is light. This light is the essence of who we are. Ironically, we often experience events that diminish or hide our light so that we are forced to go in search of it. We do our best to convince ourselves that we are wrong, bad, shameful, or ugly in some way. And yet, these labels never completely resonate. They do not cause us to open up in expansion, release, and happiness. Instead, they force us into contraction, anxiety, and depression. When we are in contraction, fear, anxiety, or depression, we are in un-truth. The truth lightens and lifts. Falsehoods create distress and anxiety. The truth creates openness and peace.

By learning what we are *not,* we eventually are forced to go in search of what we *are.* And that ultimately leads us to the truth that we are love. This is a loving that extends beyond romantic relationships, family relationships, and friendships, into the very heart of God. This is a loving that is so strong and so gentle that once you tap into it you can never walk away from it again. The first step to finding this love is acknowledging that you did nothing wrong and that every painful experience provides you with the opportunity to know an even deeper loving in your life.

What Is Soul Energy?
I use the term "Soul" to describe the part of us that is immortal. Different spiritual and religious traditions define Soul differently. You don't have to have experienced a

spiritual awakening the way I did to feel or hear your Soul. I've also felt my Soul in quiet moments that catch me off-guard where I am suddenly awash with a feeling of deep peace. For example, sometimes I feel my Soul when I'm looking out at the rain on a cozy fall day with a mug of cinnamon tea warming my hands. A nourishing feeling will take over my body and I feel this peace that seems to connect me to something deep and transcendent inside of myself. I also feel Soul when I'm in the middle of the mountains or dancing by the ocean. I can feel Soul when I'm talking to someone and we bypass the superficial level of chit-chat and drop into a deeper energy where, on some level, we just feel each other without saying a word. Soul feels like an energy that goes beyond my five senses of taste, touch, smell, hearing, and seeing. It feels like a sacred energy that connects me to something greater. When I am feeling Soul energy moving through me, I feel completely calm, safe, and connected to a deep, comforting energy.

In times of great despair, I have called upon my Soul for guidance. My Soul rarely responds in words, but I do receive help. It may come as a sign or a synchronicity or just a feeling. Sometimes help comes immediately, sometimes not. The Soul feels like a very loving presence that helps to guide my life when I allow it to. Soul is what we feel most deeply inside of us. It feels like true home, true Source. Soul is the energy that is bigger than our human egos and connects us to our divinity. It is our wise, loving, and immortal presence that speaks to us subtly in the quiet moments of our lives. Soul is what gives us that gentle nudge to pursue one path over the other. It can feel like intuition, expansion, or simply a profound sense of connection to a deeper part of our self.

Soul Exercise #1: Connecting with Your Soul

Take out your journal and write about your experiences of Soul. When have you felt your Soul? Did your Soul come to you with words, as a feeling, or in a different way? If you've never felt connected to your Soul, what do you imagine it would feel like? Imagining in this way opens the brain to new possibilities. This is the first step to actually connecting with your Soul.

I invite you to draw, paint, or sculpt your Soul. Art connects us to the more unconscious parts of our psyches where our Soul resides. If you decide to do art, which I highly encourage, don't worry about what it looks like. You want to bypass the logical brain as much as possible and let your raw creativity help lead you into an understanding of Soul. The information contained in your artwork might surprise you.

You Create from Soul

I want to pause briefly and discuss a popular saying in new age circles. You have probably heard the phrase, "you create your own reality." I want to address a few of the problems with this adage, because I have seen it do some harm, at times creating the false beliefs that lead us away from our Soul. Many people who study spirituality assume that they have done something wrong if they encounter challenging or difficult circumstances in their lives. They believe that if we can create our own realities then what is happening to them must be their fault, but this type of message actually comes from the little human self, or the ego. From this vantage point, creating our own reality means that our negative experiences are our fault, that we willed them into our lives through our bad thinking. This is not true. Remember, *you didn't do anything wrong.*

The little human self, or *ego,* sees the world around it through the lenses of blame and shame. It looks at the world and wants to know who or what is to blame for its circumstances. Often, the little human self decides that she is most at fault. I've seen many people fall into the trap of blaming themselves for some of the hard experiences they've had on Earth. Even more, I've seen many people blame themselves for the suffering they are witnessing around them on Earth. When we find ourselves stuck in a place of blame or judgment, it's important to recognize that this is the voice of the ego and not the real truth of who we are.

As we move our awareness up into our Soul-self and use self-forgiveness to clear up shame and blame, we begin to see that who we are was never *wrong.* We may have experienced difficult events in our lives, but *we* didn't *do* anything wrong. You experienced some really tough stuff, and it was hard. But that doesn't make who you are wrong or bad.

5

Every experience we have is an opportunity to learn and cultivate new skills and wisdom. These experiences may be painful, but the real suffering comes when we judge ourselves for our experiences rather than simply experiencing them. When we judge ourselves or our lives, we create real pain that sticks in our minds and bodies and robs us of happiness and joy. Believe it or not, pain more painful when we have negative thoughts or judgments about it.

The Soul uses every experience we have as an opportunity to grow and seek wisdom. Through the Soul's eyes, who we are is never bad or wrong. When we embrace forgiveness and let go of self-blame, self-shame, and self-hatred, we step into the loving embrace of Soul.

Remember, *you* didn't do anything wrong. You didn't call the hard events upon yourself, you don't deserve the bad things that have happened to you, and you don't deserve to be punished. Every experience you have had is an opportunity to learn to love yourself and forgive yourself in a deeper way. As we love ourselves more and more, we step into what we really are: pure loving.

You are not wrong and nothing you ever did was wrong. You are so deeply right. You are right in your existence and your loving. Every experience you ever had is so you could learn how to love yourself even more. Every experience you ever had is so you can look at all of the falsehoods the world wants to project upon you – that you are worthless, ugly, shameful, stupid, imperfect, or dirty – and challenge them by bringing loving to the parts of you that haven't felt good enough. All of the false projections are clues to where we need to put our loving the most, into the tender and wounded parts inside of ourselves.

Our Souls Are Curious

Souls are so deeply curious about what human life is like. They want to know what it is to have a body and to taste strawberries, ride a bike, feel the grass with bare feet, and what it is to be in love. I have a psychologist friend who likens the Soul to being a curious little kid in a grocery store. It just wants to go in there, touch everything, knock things over, make messes, create, open up boxes of sugary cereal, and play. Our Souls come into this world and get to experiment with gravity, perceiving color, feeling the density of a body, tasting food, kissing, getting a papercut, feeling the love of friendship, having a broken heart. Our Souls get to live in a body and actually *feel* the world around them. Do you know what an amazing experience it is to simply feel? Feeling warm tea move down your throat and into your belly, the crunch of biting into a freshly picked apple, the embrace of a deep bathtub filled with bubbly fragrant water. Truly, human life is extraordinary. We get to experience this adventure called life and learn, evolve, and gain wisdom while we do it. We get to feel life *in our bodies*.

We are here to enjoy all the experiences of life -- and learn from them. At the same time, we get to go on this wonderful adventure to find the truth of who we really are. The truth of who you really are is *love*. We get to taste, touch, and feel our way into experiences that guide us into knowing that at our very essence, we are love. Your Soul came to earth so you could *feel* and *know* it is pure love. Who you are is a glorious tapestry of experiences, colors, wisdom, and learning. Underneath all of it, at your most base layer, you are simply love. All of us are on a grand adventure with many twists and turns to learn this truth.

The heartbreak and traumas of life never really touch the Soul. And when we can remove the judgments we've placed on ourselves because of life events, we are able to move back into experiencing the Soul. We begin to feel the deep and unwavering love that is at our core. Your Soul hasn't done anything wrong and neither have you. You are just on this great adventure together to learn about love.

How We Awaken

"There is a crack in everything. That's how the light gets in."—Leonard Cohen

It is the human part of us—that part of us existing in these bodies—that feels the trials and tribulations of life. The body experiences the pain of feeling like an outsider, or the disappointment of being turned down for a job, being bullied for how we look, or the broken heart when a loved one passes. The body absorbs the impact of life. The Soul just wants you to awaken. The Soul wants you to awaken to the absolute magnificence of what you are: Love.

How the Soul gets us to wake up to our true nature isn't always pleasant. That car accident you had ten years ago that changed your life forever? That was your Soul calling. That relationship you had that devastated you and left you feeling dark and depressed beyond what you could ever have imagined? Again, your Soul calling. That mystery illness that the doctors can't quite seem to diagnose or help you with? Your Soul. As painful as those experience might be, or other experiences you've had that have shaken you in some way, know that those experiences were your Soul trying to love you. Your Soul was quietly nudging you to turn in its direction. It wanted you to look up, toward its magnificent love, and touch into your deepest desires. Your Soul just wants you to return to the glorious essence of you, the pure loving and authenticity that make us who we are.

Gina was a client of mine who used some tough circumstances to grow and come back to her Soul. At the age of 36, after 13 years of marriage, Gina discovered that her husband had been having an affair with one of her closest friends. Though she had felt something was "off" in her marriage, Gina had no reason to suspect that her husband was cheating, until one day she happened to notice texts from her friend on his phone. As she read the texts between her friend and her husband, Gina was shocked by the level of physical and emotional intimacy they shared. She realized that she and her husband hadn't shared intimacy like that since before they were married. She was deeply saddened and hurt and knew she could no longer be with her husband.

Within days, Gina filed for divorce. She and her husband separated immediately, and because Gina had many family assets that she brought into the marriage, she lost a great deal of money during the divorce proceedings. While stories like Gina's are not uncommon, how she handled the betrayal and her divorce was. Gina had grounds to hate her ex-husband, to hate the injustice of what had happened to her, and even to hate God for putting her in this position. She could have gone into "victim mode" and blamed everyone else for what she had experienced, and she would have been justified in doing that. And yet, while Gina was angry about all that had happened, she came to me because she wanted to learn from her husband's betrayal and their separation. She wanted to work through the anger and the hurt and clear a lifelong pattern of being disappointed by the people closest to her.

Gina chose to use the experience of the betrayal and her divorce to grow. She wanted to use this awful, painful experience to her own benefit. In our work together, Gina began to wake up to parts of herself that she buried long ago. At one point in our work together, Gina realized that deep down, she wasn't sure she had wanted to marry her husband to begin with. She faced tremendous pressure from her family at a young age to get married and start a family. And yet, Gina had always had dreams of becoming a flight attendant, traveling the world, and having wild love affairs along the way.

As we continued to work together, it became clear that over time Gina had lost touch with her Soul's desire to travel, write about her adventures, and explore herself in various relationships. She instead succumbed to intense family pressure, got married young, and tried to live a life that never truly fit her. It became clear that Gina had betrayed herself and her dreams long before her husband ever betrayed her.

Over the course of the next few months, Gina got back in touch with her Soul's desire and began applying for jobs with airlines. She began writing about her experiences and, in doing so, connected to a deep feeling of peace inside of her. Gina started to carve out time each day to be with herself and relish the sacred. She began doing yoga. She also allowed herself an hour at the end of the day to turn off her phone, sit in her chair by the window, and enjoy a single glass of red wine in the quiet. In those calm moments, Gina could feel a deep peace and safety. She felt herself connect to a deeper part of herself. Gina began to feel happy.

As Gina and I worked together, she became increasingly in touch with her own needs. She connected to herself and her own desires for the first time since she was a teenager. She began to cultivate time in her day to actively connect to herself and feel her needs and wants.

Gina used the betrayal in her life to look at the ways she was betraying herself. In doing so, she empowered

11

herself and began attuning to the wisdom of her Soul. Her deepest Soul desire was to travel, write, and explore so Gina gave herself permission to do just that. She used her life's traumas as a means to grow and come into deeper relationship with herself. Gina used what happened to her to her own advantage. She used the hurt and pain to propel her into growth and into connecting more deeply with herself and her desires.

Instead of hating and blaming, Gina used the hard events in her life to her benefit. She found herself and connected to the deepest part of herself: her Soul. She moved into loving herself and her own life. Gina began to live from the core of herself, the Soul-connected part of herself, instead of the superficial part of herself that had previously been caught up in what everyone else wanted for her. She began to feel and live out her greatest desires.

In this way, Gina used the trauma of the betrayal and divorce to begin living her life from a place of self-love, rather than trying to fit into the mold of the culture around her. In a strange way, the hard experiences she had broke her open so she could be truly free to connect to herself and live the life she really wanted.

As Gina's story illustrates, sometimes we experience really difficult events so we can go in search of our truth. Like a broken bone that heals stronger, life's wounding often leads us into our places of greatest strength. Gina was able to re-connect to her deepest desires and she found the strength to actually pursue them. In this way, Gina used the most challenging experience of her life to awaken to her most authentic self. She used the trauma of her husband's and friend's betrayal to propel her into excavating her deepest dreams. And for the first time since childhood, Gina began to feel the wild ecstatic happiness of desires fulfilled.

Last we spoke, Gina had been hired at a major airline to work as a check-in agent. With the free flights she has through her job, Gina has started to travel around the world and has even started a blog chronicling her adventures to Europe, Mexico, Costa Rica, and Australia. Gina started to step into the dating world again and reported to me that she is learning how to have fun with men, receive, and trust herself. She said she is finally living the kind of life she imagined for herself when she was a young girl, and most of all, she feels happy.

This is the Soul's magic. It sends events into your life to change your life, mix you up, and ultimately transform the tragedy and challenges into loving. The Soul wants to be your guide, your Source, and your home. The ability to tap into and feel your Soul — and to understand everything it has done for you in its mission to wake you up to love — that is awakening. The Soul knows there is a great plan for you and it conspires to get you on the path of loving, ease, and fulfillment. Life's greatest tragedies are often the vehicle the Soul uses to wake us up to the deepest, most real, parts of ourselves so that we can experience true loving and bliss.

As we grow and experience heartaches, heart breaks, loving, loss of loving, sorrow, pain, disappointment, joy, happiness, elation, and self-doubt, we form our personal history. The moments of happiness and joy we're not going to touch. There is no need to heal those — they are gifts of living. But those moments that weren't so easy, those moments that made you shut down inside, even if just a little, those are the moments we are going to remedy with loving. We are going to use those moments to your advantage so you can find a deeper love and connection to yourself than ever before.

We Are Love

> "They say there's only love or fear, but there's really only love. Sometimes it takes being afraid a while to see that."—Brian Andreas, writer

Our home is love. We came from love, and to love we shall return. When I say love, I am not talking about romantic love. I am talking about a love that is so deep and so true that it cannot be taken away, it cannot be destroyed, and it cannot be tainted. I am talking about cosmic, or universal, love. You can call it the love of God, or the love of the Soul, or the love of the Universe. This is the loving that is always present to us and always available to us. It isn't dependent on another person or being loving us. Indeed, personal romantic love and familial love is all part of this big cosmic love. However, we often mistake romantic love or family love *for* cosmic love. Sometimes it is; sometimes it isn't. Cosmic love is so gentle, so sweet, you'll want to bathe in it for hours. It isn't about one person or one thing. It is about love for the sake of loving. I see it as a beautiful pink, golden, cloud of light that lifts us on the gentlest of pillows. There is the sweetest feeling you've ever felt when you tap into cosmic love.

When I first experienced cosmic love, it was in a meditation I am going to share with you shortly. I imagined this pink golden light surrounding me and filling up every hole, every wound in my body. After this meditation, I was filled with so much energy that for seven days straight, I had to go on a run (and let me tell you, I am not a runner). There was so much energy and love coursing through my body that I felt as if I had no choice but to express it through running sprints in the mountains! The energy eventually integrated and my career as a runner ended shortly after, but I will never forget the profound and intense experience that was tapping into cosmic love.

Since then, I have a feeling of cosmic love being this golden field of energy in which we are all sitting. It surrounds us at all times, only we don't always see it or feel it. Before this experience of feeling cosmic love, I only felt love when in relationship with another human being or animal. I felt love from boyfriends, young children, parents, and pets. I thought love was only felt when two beings loved each other.

But after this meditation experience, I could see that love is an energy field we are all in all of the time. When we share a loving moment with another person, we are tapping into that greater field of love. I'm a person who loves to cuddle and one of my favorite activities is to have my husband hold me while we watch a television show or before we fall asleep. I feel so safe, warm, cared for, and loved when he has his arms around me. And yet, I also know that he isn't the source of love. In those moments where we get to hold each other, we get to have a tangible and embodied experience of shared love, and it is wonderful. And yet, he isn't the source of love. For both of us, our source of love comes from God, Soul, Universe, or whatever word you prefer to use to describe the divine intelligence that runs through us all. We get to just express it with each other in ways that feel comforting and sweet. When two people get to express their love for each other in some way, they are tapping into and expressing from the expansive field of love that we all live in and is always present to us.

If you've ever had experiences of touching that kind of cosmic love, great. If not, you get to go on the tremendously rewarding journey of finding it. Here is one thing I know: You will find it. I cannot say how or when — t may be because of reading this book. It may be from something else completely. But your destiny is to find the loving again. Your destiny is to feel the expansive love that surrounds you and runs through you at all times. We don't have to go in search of love, we are already living inside of more love than we can possibly imagine.

♥

Soul Exercise #2: Feeling Cosmic Love*

This is a meditation to help you touch into what cosmic love feels like.

1) Make yourself comfortable.
2) I invite you to close your eyes if that feels good to you.
3) Take a few deep breaths and just let go of your day.
4) Imagine your body being surrounded and filled by a soft pink light. This is a gentle light that just bathes your body in a way that feels comforting and loving.
5) Watch this pink light fill any holes or wounds in your body and heart. It just softly touches these places.
6) Do this for as long as it feels good; I recommend at least 10 minutes.
7) I invite you to journal about this experience. What was it like for you?

Through this exercise, you may get a taste of what cosmic or Universal love feels like. You can also tap into a feeling of this kind of love by just imagining someone in your life who has loved you unconditionally. Spirit often loves us through the people in our lives who are able to love us completely and totally.

* Adapted from a meditation in *Eyes Made of Soul* by Dr. Robert Waterman.

How We Forget Our Love

You might have forgotten that you are, quite simply, love. You come from love, you are love, and you will return to love. Life has a funny way of helping us forget this truth. When hard moments hit, it can feel like we are hurt, angry, or suffering instead of love. The core essence of you, however, is still love. It gets masked temporarily by life's ups and downs. When we encounter tough times, we often identify with our reactions to them. We think we *are* the sadness, rage, or fear that we are experiencing, but they are only emotions. The truth is, you are still love.

There was a Ben & Jerry's ice cream that reminded me of this concept. It was a new flavor they were introducing that had a cookie core inside it. My boyfriend at the time had bought a pint of their peanut-butter chocolate ice cream with a fudge cookie core. When you opened the lid, you could see this core of dark chocolate fudge cookie running through the very center of the ice cream all the way to the bottom of the container. The vanilla peanut butter ice cream surrounded it. You were supposed to eat the ice cream by taking a bite of the cookie core with the ice cream.

The loving of our being is like that cookie core. There is a core of love that runs through us. Sometimes all we can feel or taste is the surrounding peanut butter ice cream, but, nevertheless, that cookie core is always there. The core of who we are is simply pure love, but we forget as we get temporarily swept up in negative emotions like hurt, fear, and anger.

We are here to love and accept ourselves, which returns us to living from that cookie core. We are here to unplug from all of the ways we've depended on other people for our sense of worthiness, love, and belonging and to plug into ourselves instead. We are here to shower ourselves with adoration, gentleness, kindness, and forgiveness. When we do, it moves us straight into the heart of God and we get to live from the core truth of who we are: Love. We bypass the conflict, drama, and turmoil of life on earth and head straight into the loving that fills us and nurtures us at our deepest level.

As we move into living from our loving core, it doesn't mean that the love we have with families, friends, and lovers disappears. Quite the opposite. When we start to tap into our own loving and stop needing others to love us in order to feel okay and fulfilled, our relationships often blossom into an even greater depth of loving.

I've seen this occur countless times in my practice. One client I had, Nancy, came to me after a string of heartbreaks. She was 42 years old and had about two decades of various failed relationships under her belt. She would meet men, they would fall madly in love with her, and they would quickly make promises about the future. They would often take her on vacations or buy her expensive gifts. However, after a few months, they would disappear, usually without a word to her as to why. They would abruptly stop calling or texting.

After a particularly passionate affair that again left Nancy heartbroken and confused, she found me. During our first call, I had a sense that someplace deep in her past, Nancy was abandoned by a caregiver. When I asked her about this, she said yes, she was. She had never really thought of it, but when she was four years old, her father had to leave to work overseas. Though her parents remained married and her Dad would return home a couple of times a year, somewhere deep inside Nancy felt abandoned. Later, her logical adult self knew that her Dad decided to work overseas in order to better financially support Nancy and her mother. However, a young part of Nancy thought she was responsible for sending her father away. *This young part of her decided that any man she loved would always leave.*

This created a false belief that unconsciously guided Nancy's future. It was a belief that was created so young Nancy didn't even realize it was there until I brought it to her attention. Once she was aware of it, I had Nancy repeat the phrase, "I forgive myself for judging myself for believing that men I love will always leave." I had Nancy take a deep breath and then asked her what she experienced in her body. She said she felt a lightness and a softness around her heart area and that she felt a renewed sense of optimism. She said she no longer felt hopeless. It was in that moment that Nancy began to re-center into the core of her true self. She began to release her identification as someone who is abandoned and returned to the truth of the loving that she inherently embodies. Nancy returned to her core.

Later in our work, I had Nancy go back and do some forgiveness directly with her inner four-year-old. In that process, Nancy began to cry and release 38 years of pain and hurt. I guided her into giving her inner four-year-old everything that that four-year-old wanted and needed but never received. We went back in time and nurtured and attended to that four-year-old in all of the ways Nancy had wanted from her father. In doing this, Nancy was able to reclaim the love that she had given away to her father as a young child and bring it back to herself. This again helped her to return to the essential loving that was at her core.

As young children, we depend on our caregivers for love, support, and nurturing. When one parent leaves, either intentionally or not, part of our love goes with them. When this occurs, we lose part of our wholeness. When we go back and forgive ourselves for any false beliefs and love that inner young child, we bring our love back home to ourselves. And this is where our love truly belongs.

If we grow up in a household where our caregivers are able to provide all of the nurturing and loving we need, we internalize that love and grow up feeling relatively whole. It is when that process is interrupted for some reason that we need to go back and give ourselves the loving and support that was halted. Doing that restores our loving. We can retrieve our love from all of the places outside of ourselves where we've tried to store it for safekeeping

Nancy had forgiven herself for the false belief she created as a child and began to love herself. She loved the inner four-year-old in the way that she had craved and needed at the time. Doing so restored the interrupted nurturing Nancy had experienced growing up. I also encouraged Nancy to love herself as she is now. We talked about all of the physical acts of nurturing she could provide for herself to show her Soul that she was committed and devoted to nurturing herself. Nancy began walking her dog in the morning and relished the silence of twilight. She bought herself a few items of clothing that felt soft and comforting to her skin. And she began making regular date nights with herself where she would put on a favorite movie, enjoy one of the specialty cupcakes from a neighborhood bakery, and paint her nails a light bubble pink that truly delighted her. Nancy began to genuinely love herself, releasing the self-judgment she had been carrying around for 38 years, and devoted herself to herself.

After doing this work and re-aligning with her loving core, Nancy e-mailed me a few months after our last session and told me she had met an amazing man. She was proceeding slowly with him but already something felt different. She no longer expected to be abandoned, so it changed her behavior in the relationship as well as the type of man she chose to date. A year and a half later, she sent me their wedding photo. As Nancy forgave herself for the ways she created false beliefs and tended to and nurtured herself, she aligned with her loving core. She no longer needed a man to fill the emotional holes inside of her. She had filled them with her own loving and nurturing. And in doing so, she was finally able to create a loving partnership that was based on sharing, fun, and play. When she began to truly love herself, loving expanded from her core out into her external life.

Learning to plug into your own loving will only create more loving in your life, not less.

The Loving Truth

Are you ready for an experience of loving? A loving so deep and sweet that it may be unlike anything you've ever felt? This is the loving that is at the core of you but may have been covered up by life's ups and downs. Are you ready for a life that is easier? Begin with the concept that you have never done anything wrong and feel the weight within your heart begin to lighten.

No expression of God has ever been wrong. You have never been wrong. Nothing in your life has been a mistake. It has all been learning. We are all here to walk our own paths, reclaim our lost parts, and find our own loving.

You are valuable and so deeply worthy. The value of your brilliance, or your gifts, may have been misunderstood or even rejected. But I'm here to tell you, who you are isn't wrong —the truth is that who you are is incredible. You are hearing these words and the part of you that exists in the bottom of your being, the very depths, remembers this truth. That you, beloved, are sacred. That you are precious. Let's help you remember this truth.

Chapter 2
Climbing Out of the Swamp and into the Meadow

As we move through life, we encounter hard times. That is the nature of life here on earth, and it isn't a problem in and of itself, because we often grow from our challenges and painful situations. We only run into problems when we use those experiences to form opinions and judgments about ourselves that aren't true—when we use our life experiences against ourselves. What happens to us only becomes an issue when we use it to decide that we are unworthy or unlovable in some way.

The truth is, through all of these events, we learn. We learn about ourselves, we learn about our relationships, and we learn about our needs. We are on this planet to evolve and to awaken. We often do that through difficult experiences that ultimately lead us to know who we are and what we really need and desire.

Do You Feel Stuck?

Growing up in this culture, we all endure negative events.
However, we are rarely taught how to integrate these
difficult experiences into our lives and heal them so that
we can move on from them. We are not taught how to
work through our traumas and release them, so instead we
often get stuck. We will suffer through a difficult, hurtful,
or painful situation and our heart will break a little bit. It
will hold onto that pain, or anger, or rage. Our hearts need
a little coaching about how to move through the pain and
to the other side. Life can be seen as a long journey. In
that journey, we travel through gorgeous fields, meadows,
streams, and, at times, deep and dark canyons with swamps
at the bottom. Too often, when we descend into a canyon,
we get stuck in the swamp. We want to climb out of the
canyon and back into the sunlight on the other side, but we
don't know how. We lose our map, we lose our direction,
and we lose our way.

We all encounter traumas, challenges, and difficulties
at some point in our lives. They may be major; they may
be minor. But they all have an effect. One of my clients,
Ashlee, came to me with severe anxiety and panic attacks.
She had three miscarriages in the past three years and she
was traumatized by each one and convinced they were
her fault. Another client of mine, Paula, came to me after
experiencing some severe health issues. She had gone into
her local hospital to give birth to her son and needed a
C-section. During the procedure, bacteria entered her gut

that wound up causing her tremendous gastro-intestinal problems for years to come. Another client of mine, Tom, found me to work on the pain and heartbreak he felt from being adopted. His trauma manifested as addiction to alcohol because he couldn't seem to process the pain of feeling abandoned as a newborn. Each one of these clients had formed false beliefs after the difficult incident they had experienced. Ashlee had unknowingly adopted the belief "I've lost my chance to be a mother." Paula had created the belief "My body is my enemy." Tom held the false belief "I am inherently unlovable." All three of these people had experienced trauma and then created a false belief around it.

Since we are human, hardships like this seem inevitable. We spend our lives trying to avoid the pain and trauma of experiences like these. However, I want to tell you that trauma doesn't have to ruin your life, ruin your joy, or ruin your happiness. In a way, trauma is just a part of being human. The key is that we haven't been taught how to deal with it. We aren't taught how to forgive ourselves for what we've been through. And, as a result, we aren't taught how to excavate the real self, the gorgeous essence of you, from the rubble of pain and difficulties. We are not taught how to clear up these events — or rather, the dysfunctional beliefs we adopted as a result of these events. We are not taught how to get out of that swamp and back to our essence.

The good news is, there are new maps. There are directions for how to get out of that swamp and back into the beautiful meadow. New brain research is revealing there are techniques that can help re-wire the brain. Advances in neuroscience are helping us create better and better ways of helping people out of the dark canyons and back into the sunlight by gently tending to our traumas. You do not have to remain stuck forever. Trauma does not have to haunt you for the rest of your life.

Shame Keeps Us Stuck

Trauma causes the most harm when it instills a sense of shame inside of us. Many of these hard events that occur can make us feel bad about ourselves. Guilt is created when we believe we've *done* something bad. Shame forms when we believe we *are* bad. When we experience a difficult event or someone says something mean or hurtful to us, it can make us question our worth. Something inside of us starts to feel bad or dirty. This is shame. Shame is dangerous because it attacks your sense of worth. The lie it tells you is that you aren't enough.

However, the events you've endured and the messages you received growing up were never actually about you. They might have felt like they were, but they were really others' projections. People may have said mean things to you or behaved cruelly, but that was their own shame they were taking out on you. It wasn't about you. When we feel shame and don't heal it, we try to put it on other people and make them carry the shame instead. I had a professor in my Master's program who told us, "victims take on the shame of their perpetrators." Shame is such an unpleasant feeling that many people try to cast out their own shame by shaming others. It is truly a tragic cycle.

However, there is a way to end the cycle and that is through exposing shame to love. Shame can only exist when it hides. It thrives on secrecy. You were asked to carry shame. You were told it was the truth of who you are and what you deserved. But that was a lie. And if you experienced a traumatic event where someone made you feel ashamed, it is likely keeping you stuck in pain.

Please allow the shame that was placed inside you to dissolve. It isn't yours. Expose it to the sunlight, and don't allow it to remain a secret. Don't take it in or believe it is the truth of who you are, because it is not. Shame is a virus that got planted early, inside of you. But it is *not* you. You are a divine being of love and wonder. You simply forgot. Whoever made you feel shame is also a divine being of love and wonder, but they forgot, too.

You can begin to heal your shame by first acknowledging its presence. We spend so much time and energy trying to bury shame, but when we can look at it and really feel where it exists in our bodies, we bring it out of hiding and expose it to the love of our own hearts. It can then begin dissolving. And the more we expose it to our love and the love of other safe and unconditionally loving people, the more that shame dissolves.

The Negative Leads us to the Positive

There is a spiritual reason we are immersed in so much negativity and shame in this culture. From the Soul's perspective, we are often confronted with the negative so that we can find the positive — it is one of the ways we learn and grow. Challenges force us to find inner capacities like strength, love, and compassion that we didn't know we had. I can think of a time in my own life when I was in a very difficult relationship that ultimately helped me heal parts of myself that needed healing. I was deeply in love with this man but he wasn't sure he wanted a future with me. I spent three years working on the relationship, moving to another state to be with him, and hoping he would fully commit because deep down I knew we had a special connection. However, despite all of my attempts to love this man, he pushed me away.

It was a difficult experience that caused me extreme anxiety. The thought of leaving the man I had loved more than anyone, the house we had bought, and the home we had created, caused me such angst and heartache. However, it reached a point where the anxiety, stress, and depression I felt from being pushed away was too much. The intense negativity of the situation forced me to find an inner strength I didn't know I had. It felt like I was a pressure cooker of stress and pain. Finally, the pressure got to be too high and it forced me to look inside at all of the reasons I was staying with a man who didn't want to commit fully to me. I found a strength at the very bottom of my Soul to leave the situation. After I left, I had to closely examine all of the ways my feelings of unworthiness contributed to me staying in what was an emotionally abusive situation. I found places deep within me where I still felt unworthy of a partner who could love me unconditionally and commit to me. When I did healing work on those parts, I cleared that pattern -- and attracted an incredible man who later became my husband.

Experiencing the pain and turmoil of that relationship enabled me to find a deep strength inside me that I know can never be taken away. It was also the heartbreak of losing that relationship that forced me to go deep inside of myself and find places where I still felt unworthy. Once I found and loved those parts, I attained the loving relationship I had always dreamed of.

Looking back, I can be thankful for that dramatic and painful relationship because it made me heal some parts of myself that were still hidden to me at the time. It helped me develop an internal strength so that now I am unwilling to compromise myself or tolerate emotional abuse of any kind. As painful as that relationship was, it led me into something incredibly positive. I got to heal parts of myself, find my strength, and ultimately create an even deeper loving relationship. I was able to discover an even deeper level of love for myself, which has brought more loving from friends and family, more joy, and more abundance into my life. This is how life works. Often the negative events we experience are here to lead us into the positive. They are here to help us find undiscovered gifts in ourselves. Sometimes the Soul sets up challenges for ourselves so we can fully actualize our greatest gifts.

When we really face the negative, we can see that it is positivity in disguise. Negativity is positivity that is trying to find itself again. The hard stuff leads us to finding the most wonderful parts of ourselves; it helps point us to the strength of loving inside. We find our greatest gifts when we've walked through the brandishing fire.

The hard stuff always leads us into the good stuff. We just have to be willing to use whatever happens in life to uplift ourselves, strengthen, and go deeper into loving ourselves. You will always find your way out of the canyon and swamp; sometimes it can just take a while. However, everything eventually leads us back home, to our own loving.

Again, it may not look like it or feel like it at the time. In the Dark Night of the Soul when we are stuck in that swamp, we may not see hope or love — we may even forget that this energy called "love" exists. When we've lost our way, it is easy to forget that we will always be called forth into better versions of ourselves. We may forget that sunlight and meadows and wildflowers even exist. It may take time, it may take help, it may take desperate prayer. But our lives are designed to bring us into greater levels of awareness, freedom, and love. No matter what you are going through, you will eventually be delivered back into greater strength, love, and wisdom.

And if you forget this in the tough moments, it's okay. If you've forgotten this your entire life, that's okay, too. The techniques I'm going to teach you will help you remember your truth – that you are a gorgeous being of love who is capable of deep joy and bliss. I will show you how to move out of the negative and into the positive. The wonderful truth is that often when we find the positive lesson life is trying to teach us, we no longer need the negative situation, and it can change or transform. When we find the gift of a tough event, or challenging relationship, we no longer need that event or person in the same way. Our relationship to it changes, and either that situation changes, or we simply feel free. When we stop judging ourselves, a situation, or an experience, we can begin to find the gifts.

Resolution Leads to Love

Love is the grand homecoming and, despite the difficulties we face that can overwhelm us, we are here to remember and wake up to the love that is our true essence. Every experience leads us back to love if we follow that experience through to its resolution. If we haven't found our way back to loving, then the experience isn't complete. Love is where we came from and it is where we will return. Experiences of the good, the bad, and the ugly ultimately come in to point us back to loving. If you haven't been able to find the loving in a situation, then you are still on your journey. Know that one day you will find the loving and that journey will be complete.

Tough human experiences aren't wrong. They exist side by side with joy, wonder, excitement, passion, and happiness. We might strive to live our lives with as much happiness and joy as possible, but life has a funny way of throwing us curveballs. So, if you find yourself in a state of sadness or hurt or anger, that's okay. That is your Soul helping you to work something out so you can come to know yourself in a deeper way or find qualities in yourself that you never knew you had. Each challenge brings a gift. They aren't accidents, and they aren't here to destroy us or otherwise work against us. The experiences we have in life are here to serve us if we listen to them. Each one is here to carry us into greater loving and to greater connection with our true self, the loving spiritual essence that we all are.

I had one client, Linda, who developed a serious infection in her stomach. In the course of our work together, we uncovered how, as a child, Linda had to eat foods she didn't want to because her mother would cry and yell at her in frustration if she didn't. It wasn't a surprise then that Linda found herself with a serious gut infection at age 40. As we worked together, Linda was able to heal the part of herself that was never seen or acknowledged by her mother. She worked to heal all of the parts of her that believed that to be loved she had to do things that weren't in alignment with her true self. As a young child, Linda was sensitive, intuitive, and creative. However, her mother never saw these gifts in Linda and instead yelled at her for being too sensitive and too picky. In this instance, her mother's need to feel like a good mother (so she could feel worthy) trumped Linda's actual needs.

As an adult, Linda was always confused about her own needs. She married an alcoholic man and her entire focus was on keeping him happy, so he wouldn't yell at their children. As Linda embarked on her healing journey, she was able to see how as a young child she was never understood and gave away her needs and then married a man who never understood her and demanded she give up her needs again. As she began to understand herself, she remembered her intuitive and empathic nature. During her healing journey, Linda even discovered some latent healing gifts inside of herself. With time, Linda was able to heal her gut infection. As a result, she was able to step into her own right as a healer. Linda is now divorced and has a healing practice where she helps other people with her gifts. Linda finally feels happy.

In this case, Linda's journey through the dark (growing up never being seen, the alcoholic husband, and gut infection) helped her to uncover gifts that were buried inside of her. Her healing gifts were within her all along, but it took turmoil to shake them loose and bring them to the surface. As Linda deepened in her love for herself, she became self-confident and in touch with her own needs. She was able to love herself for the first time, and as a result she was able to create a life that brings her happiness and joy.

Other clients of mine have walked similar journeys of finding the gifts in the hard challenges they have encountered. Samantha was a doctor who experienced extreme anxiety every time she walked into the hospital where she worked. When we looked deeper into her anxiety, we found that it was trying to teach her that it was safe to love the patients she attended. The anxiety occurred when Samantha was concerned with being the "perfect" doctor, which to her meant abandoning her emotions and love. In our work together, she learned to see the anxiety as an indicator that she could bring loving with her into the hospital and into every patient interaction. As a result, Samantha began to love her job. The anxiety became a reminder that Samantha had forgotten that love was the most important aspect of her job. And so, Samantha began to use the anxiety as a cue to remind her that her loving was enough and that any medical interventions she did were just pragmatic.

Another client of mine, John, came to me in a state of extreme spiritual emergency. He was having horrific nightmares and experienced crippling anxiety while at work. As we worked together, we saw there were parts of himself that he had judged as bad, wrong, and unworthy. These parts were coming to him in his dreams and figuratively chasing him down in what felt like terrible nightmares. When John confronted the parts of himself that he had neglected and judged, he found healing. The anxiety subsided and he was able to do his job. John had to learn to forgive himself for casting aside parts of himself that he thought were shameful and unworthy. As he did this, he discovered a love for himself that was so deep and rewarding he was able to move into a happy relationship and fulfilling career.

A New Dawn

What comes into our lives is here to teach us and to help us uncover parts of ourselves that might have been buried. A hard circumstance shows us where we need to love ourselves. The areas in which we feel the most stress signal to us where we need to love ourselves the most. These are often the places where we feel most unworthy. Our job is to dive in and reclaim our sense of worthiness. As we undo those false beliefs and self-judgments we've placed on ourselves, we unleash our Soul essence, which is the foundation of true happiness and joy.

What happens in our lives truly is here to serve us. Things don't happen *to* us; they happen *for* us. What has happened to you isn't *wrong.* You just haven't known how to heal it and use whatever happened to your own advantage. Who you are never was and never will be wrong — only your beliefs about yourself may be wrong. You are so deeply right on every level. If you are brave enough to confront the places inside you that feel heavy, ashamed, and stuck, you will be led into freedom.

Chapter 3
Finding the Source of Our Hurt

Personal difficulties are likely to occur throughout our lifetimes. All of us — it doesn't matter what family you are from, where you grew up, who your parents were, or where you went to school — have experienced adversity of some kind. It is what we are here to do so we can learn and evolve and come to really and truly know ourselves. Each and every one of us endures hardship and challenges in some way. We can't escape the human experience of grief, loss, hurt, and sadness. We don't need to. We don't need to resist them or run away from them. All we need to do is learn how to work with them — and work through them.

In this chapter we'll examine how and when some of our negative beliefs get formed, usually during early painful experiences that often reach back into childhood. You will learn how the negative feelings surrounding these events remain buried inside of you (and can be released). I will share some important soul exercises with you so that you can find the source of your hurt and begin your healing journey.

We Are Born Connected to the Spirit World

If you've ever had children or worked with children, you'll notice that babies come into this world with an openness and sense of wonder. There is something so innocent and pure about them. They have a natural, effortless joy and are easily delighted. Many of us believe babies are still connected to the spirit world. Remember that you were once open, innocent, and connected to other worlds. You, too, were a magical baby, playing with spirits, angels, and feeling the love of God in your belly and heart. There are countless stories of children who are able to see what the adults around them cannot. Indeed, very young children are connected to the heart of God.

Around age six or seven, something begins to change. In their desire to be accepted and included, children of this age start to notice that they need to be a certain way to fit in and be liked. They feel social pressure to be normal and have friends. To do this, many children abandon their connection to God and try to connect to the physical world around them instead. They start trying to belong. They also begin to receive more messages about what they *should* do and how they *should* behave in order to fit in and be normal. Creativity begins to diminish. I remember being six years old, playing in the sandbox at my school, aware that I was different, somehow not part of the bigger group of children.

And it felt awful. I can distinctly remember the time in my life when I began consciously choosing to try to fit in a little more. Most children do this around six or seven years old. As a result, at this tender age, we start to lose our innocence and wonder. Part of us begins to harden as we become more and more a part of this world.

By ages eight and nine, we've lost most of our connection to the young wonder child we once were. We are more acclimatized to the world around us and less in touch with our own essence and wonder. Children at this age start to look more grown up, less like children. Their innocence begins to wane. Children who could once see spirits, and may have talked with angels, usually stop doing so at this point. And this is part of the human path. As we grow up, we lose touch with that sweet, innocent part of us that came into this world full of love and who was so connected to God. Around ages eight or nine, most children begin to harden slightly. All of this occurs largely unconsciously.

Over time, this hardening continues. As we grow, we increasingly lose touch with that wild and wondrous self who was so open to the world and so linked to the heart of God. As we enter school, our connection to our wonderful mystical young self nearly, if not totally, vanishes. The very way our educational system works, with its emphasis on logic, math, science, and production, helps to bury the wonder child underground.

Our First Heart Wounds

We live in a culture that values logic, reason, and empiricism. The young wonder child has no use for and no experience with these things. She is often taught to abandon her daydreams, her fantasy, her play, and her joy in favor of arithmetic and reading. She gets indoctrinated into a culture that believes connection to joy and the unseen worlds is useless. We are taught to move from our bodies and our hearts into our minds. As children, we are even taught that the unseen worlds don't exist and are make believe. We are trained early on to abandon the part of us that knows how to play, how to create, how to commune with other beings, how to rest in our hearts, and how to find joy. This is usually the first heart wound we ever experience.

These early wounds are some of the most powerful heart wounds we experience, because they are our first big wounds and they occur when our energy bodies are more open. Many people spend their lives trying unconsciously to heal the heart wounds that formed when they were young. I've seen time and time again working with clients that early childhood, elementary school, middle school, and high school are when we experience our deepest pain.

It is a culturally sanctioned trauma that we all undergo when we are forced out of our spirit, heart, and imagination and into the mental realm. In addition, life events and personal traumas that occur at that time are some of the most impactful we ever experience. When we are young, we are still figuring out the world and how it works. And, so, novel events that we experience go into our brain's catalogue of "how the world is" and "how the world works." If we experience an event in our childhood, we use it as a data point to form beliefs about ourselves and the world.

Thus, these events that happen to us when we are young take on the most significance over the course of our lives. For example, I had a client, Mattie, who grew up in a family that did not have much money. Her father worked in a factory in the Midwest, and her mother stayed at home with Mattie and her three siblings. Mattie was a highly sensitive child, and her mother told her that she had always enjoyed drawing and staring off into space. When Mattie went to kindergarten, she was at once singled out and teased by her peers for her tattered clothing and tendencies to space out while on the playground. They would call her "poor," "weird," and "ugly." These words deeply impacted Mattie. In her first experience of the world outside of her family unit, she was met with classmates who mocked her for the old hand-me-downs she was wearing and her natural tendencies to live in her imagination.

At that time, Mattie began to become preoccupied with how she looked. She would go home and cry to her mother and beg for new clothes, so that she wouldn't be the target of so much playground teasing. Mattie stopped daydreaming the way she once did. She still drew, but her drawings went from wild fantasies about other planets and worlds to drawings that resembled her classmates' drawings of their houses and families. In essence, it was at this time that Mattie started to close down her wonder child and her deep connection to her own Spirit and Soul. In a way, she had to do that to survive the teasing and bullying around her. Yet, in doing so, Mattie lost the single most important part of her: her connection to her own Spirit.

As she grew up, Mattie felt a sense of anxiety or depression that seemed to haunt her. She felt most alive when she was creating art of some kind or was out in nature. But those moments were fleeting. That early childhood experience of being so innocently open to the world and then being made fun of so deeply affected Mattie that she carried with her a sense of heaviness in almost everything she did.

During childhood, we are finding out who we are as individuals. We innately come in with open hearts and open minds. We come down to earth with such openness and such deep spiritual connection. And then, our hearts get trampled and bruised by life's events. We love others, only to have our love rejected or not returned. We love the world, only to see what pain there is around us. We grow up and get into relationships and open our hearts, only to have hurt, sorrow, and pain make their way into our beings. We love our families, only to feel their hardships, pain, or disapproval. We are told to give up our sense of spiritual connection and to use reason and logic instead.

In response to events like these, most of us have to shut down parts of ourselves to survive. The part of us that knew how to feel safe in the world may disappear deep into our heart. The part of us that trusted love may bury herself and cover herself up with rocks. We often hide our most sacred parts when we are met with our first experiences of criticism, rejection, abandonment, instability, betrayal, and neglect.

Over time, we close down our loving. We close down these hearts of ours so that the arrows of hurt, anger, fear, betrayal, and abuse don't make their way into our corporeal being. We close down to try to protect ourselves. Although heart wounds and spiritual disconnection start at a young age, they can carry into adulthood and beyond. Indeed, life seems to be about going back and reclaiming the places we were wounded and replacing them with love.

Here on earth, love can hurt. Or rather, we hurt when those around us take away their love. We feel it in our physical bodies (more on this in the next chapter). We feel those arrows of heartbreak like stabs in our gut and chest. We feel it when the people we love are suffering and we can't help them. And it hurts.

But all is not lost. Your early life and wounding doesn't destine you for a life of suffering. Our early experiences shape us and mold us — and give us amazing opportunities to get to know ourselves in an even deeper way than we ever have before. As we go back to our early years and look at the ways we've judged ourselves or created false beliefs about ourselves, we cull incredible gems of wisdom and learning. The pain we experienced moves us into greater evolution and wisdom.

Mattie and I worked together to find the core beliefs she created as a result of being teased when her heart was so wide open. We found beliefs such as *I will never be good enough, who I am is fundamentally wrong, I will never fit in,* and *I have to change myself in order to be liked and loved.* We cleared those beliefs with the forgiveness statements I will teach you. We also went back and excavated Mattie's wonder child from the heap of self-judgment and shame under which she had been buried. As a result, Mattie began to feel happy for the first time since she was five years old. She enrolled in art classes, began dressing in ways that made her feel good, and felt a sense of vibrancy and love for herself and the world that she hadn't known before.

The good news is that the wonder child can always be found again. Healing all of the ways we were made to feel "less than" while growing up can be quite simple.

Healing Your Heart

So how do we heal the heart? How do we take off our bandages, heal the bruises, and live life in a softer way? How do we tap back into loving who we really are?

The first step is to acknowledge the sweet, sensitive, intuitive child who got lost when you started to cover your heart with bandages and shields. That very young you was so sensitive and open. When she felt her first heart wounds, she started to bury herself deeper in your heart. She put up a few shields, maybe built a moat, but she told herself that she wouldn't come out until it felt safe again.

So how do we reconnect back to the original feeling? How do you help that heart heal the bruises and scars that mar its beautiful ruby prism? That is what I am here to teach you. You don't have to carry your emotional scars with you.

This young, tender version of you has been waiting for you. She has been inside you all along, perhaps visible, perhaps not. She has been waiting for the adult you, the "you" now, to go look for her, find her, and let her know that everything is okay and that she isn't alone.

I want to reconnect the two of you. Right now, we are going to go find that lost little boy or girl, who dug so deeply down into your heart that you might have forgotten she existed at all. We are going to call forth that sweet innocent little you, and let her know that even if she felt she was abandoned and rejected, she is welcome now. She is wanted. By you.

Soul Exercise #3: Meeting your Inner Child

In this exercise, I want you to call forth your inner child. Read through the five steps below and then practice them and see how you feel.

1) If it feels safe to you, close your eyes.
2) Take a few big deep breaths. Let go of your day, let go of any worries, let go of any people or concerns about the future.
3) In your mind's eye, call forth the young you, the little you. Don't overthink it. Ask her to come meet you. Let her know you are safe. Allow to appear what wants to appear. You might see a version of you when you were younger, or you might see an energy or color. If it is hard to see anything, notice if you feel her instead. If you are still having a hard time, imagine what she would look like if you could see her.
4) Notice her. What does she look like? What is she wearing? How old is she? What is she feeling? What is your sense of her?
5) Spend a couple of minutes just being with her. Let her know that she is in a safe space now. We are going to come back and talk to her a little later, but for now, I just want you to meet her.

What was that like for you? What images did you see? If it was challenging to see or sense anything, that's okay. You can imagine a photograph of your younger self instead.

When you are done, write a paragraph about what you experienced. If you feel called to journal about your experience or do some art related to it, please do. It is always an incredible experience to draw the little you. It's okay if drawing or painting isn't your thing. How your art looks doesn't matter. What matters is the feeling of connection you get when you do it.

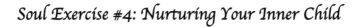

Soul Exercise #4: Nurturing Your Inner Child

Now we are going to go a bit deeper with Little You. Find a quiet place where you can sit comfortably for a few minutes for this next exercise.

1) In your mind's eye, call forth that young Little You that you just met.
2) Notice what she looks like and how she is feeling.
3) If it feels safe for both of you, call her over and let yourself hold her. Hold her as if she was your very own child. Kiss her head, hold her in your arms, love her with all your might. Hold her gently and tenderly as if she was a beloved sweet child (she is).
4) Hold her and love her for as long as it feels good. It could be a few minutes or a half hour. Take all the time you need, just loving each other. Love and nurture her in all the ways she never got or needed more of. Give her all the affection she craved at that age, letting her know that you are completely there for her.

When we are hurt, the sweet innocent part of ourselves is the first to go underground. That is our most precious and beloved part of our self. That is our divinity. Matt Kahn, a spiritual teacher, says that the inner child is the Higher Self in disguise. I agree. That sweet innocent part of our self is our highest truth; the highest expression of all that makes us wonderful. When she went underground, our very essence, joy, and light went with her. You are reclaiming your Higher Self, that loving inside of you, when you re-establish contact with little you.

Again, write a paragraph about what you felt and experienced. You can also create a piece of artwork around your experience. Reflecting on this process through writing and artwork helps to deepen your connection to the inner child. Doing so creates deeper healing.

The Healing Truth

The process of healing is the process of moving from basing your worth on external people, places, and events to your intrinsic worth as a being of love. We move from taking in the words, criticisms, and abuse of our past, and forming our identities based on that, to finding the loving within and making that our primary identity, instead. And, indeed, that is our true identity.

The events that have happened to us do not make us who we are. The bad words spoken to us do not make us who we are. The heartbreaks, disappointments, and our feelings of failure do not make us who we are. The abuses and bullying we've encountered do not actually make us who we are.

You are not the ugly, weak, worthless, or unintelligent being you might have been told you were. No. You are not shameful in any way. Any experience you had that made you believe you were was an incomplete experience. To move to completion, you have to excavate the rubble of false beliefs and internalized self-judgment on which you based your identity. Growing up you may have been made fun of for your clothes or looks, or maybe your mother told you that you needed to lose weight or your father called you stupid or incompetent. None of it is actually true. You have to move into truth. You have to complete the experience and find the wisdom you've gained. You have to move through it, back into the truth of the experience, which is that you are a gorgeous, worthy being, who is an expression of loving. Perhaps the clothes you wore as a child were precursors to you finding an incredible and enviable sense of style and creativity. Maybe your mother telling you to lose weight can be the beginning of a journey into loving your body unconditionally. If your father criticized your competency or intelligence, perhaps you can look at all the ways in which your brain thinks uniquely and can offer outside-of-the-box thoughts and solutions. All of the negatives we were told are actually positives in disguise.

The truth is, who we really are is a positive expression of loving. Our physical bodies are an expression of God. We forget this when we come to Earth. Our task, our mission, is to uncover our real truth. And once we do, we glean a tremendous amount of wisdom about the nature of our true selves and God. Once we find our loving center, our light-filled essence again, it can never be lost. Once you break your ruby heart out of the prison of falsehoods in which it has been trapped, it can never again be locked up or dulled in any way. Once you start to awaken to the truth of your being, you can't go back. The loving begins to take hold, and it transforms all those places of untruth. The loving comes in and melts the frozen false beliefs that have trapped your heart. You can begin loving and understanding yourself, and then revel in the delicious loving of your own Soul.

Tapping into our truth, and tapping into the loving of who we really are, is the most scrumptious, luscious, and comforting experience there is. Once we awaken to our loving and our truth, we awaken to the soft pink glow emanating from our Souls. We tap into a love that surpasses any human love. We tap into the very heart of God. We tap into the loving that existed before time and will exist forever — a loving and safety that can never be taken from us. Ever.

Your Soul Wants You to Find Healing

Our lives are always trying to move us into healing. Know that if you find yourself thinking about an event that was difficult, your psyche is bringing it to the surface because it wants healing. It wants to make you aware of a wound that needs attention. Your Soul is longing to mine the gift in what happened to you. So when you find yourself ruminating about a particular event in your past, know that your consciousness is seeking healing and learning. Obsessing or thinking about an event in your past informs you of an energy stuck in that event—there is still something unresolved there. Remember, there is nothing wrong with you. Sometimes, we just need a little help in healing and in discovering the learning.

Here's the good news about healing: You don't need to force anyone else in your life to be a certain way before you can heal. You don't need to yell at, or change, the teachers, parents, peers, and partners who have hurt you or contributed to your disengaging from the heart of All That Is. You don't need their apology, though that can often be nice. You don't even need to forgive them, if that doesn't feel right.

Your healing isn't dependent on anyone else, or what they might have done to you. Healing happens within you, for you, and by you. Healing happens when we learn to love those places within us that feel neglected, abandoned, unsafe, or unworthy. Healing happens when we resolve the energetic block created by trauma and return to our loving essence. You don't need the people who have harmed you, whether intentionally or unintentionally, to change, accept responsibility, ask for forgiveness, or apologize. If they do, great. It can be a profoundly healing experience to have someone who has harmed you apologize with sincerity -- and vice versa. But it isn't necessary for healing. You are all that is necessary for healing. Loving, accepting, and forgiving you.

♥

Soul Exercise #5: Clearing Unresolved Events from Your Past

In this exercise, we are going to begin clearing out the trauma from difficult events in your past. This is deeply powerful work that can often be life-changing. We will be using the ancient Hawaiian technique of *ho'oponopono*. *Ho'oponopono* was used by Hawaiian shamans, or kahuna, to settle political discord between families and tribes. It is a process of reconciliation and it literally means "to make things right." Using this technique on parts of ourselves that have been split off, judged, or traumatized is a way to make our inner world right. I've found this process alone to be profound for clients. Make sure you have a space that is quiet so you can fully immerse yourself in this exercise.

1) Make a list of two or three times in your past that were difficult, traumatic, or challenging in some way. For example, it could be a time when you were bullied or teased, a time when someone you loved left or died, or a time when you experienced heartbreak of some kind. For example, I've done this process with my fifth-grade self who was bullied for being chubby and nerdy. Other clients of mine have used it for times when they went through something deeply difficult like a divorce, death of a loved one, betrayal, abuse, etc.

2) Take one of the events from your list and close your eyes. What age were you during that event? Call forward that version of you from that time. Look at her. What do you notice? What is she wearing? How is she feeling?

3) Look this version of you from the past in the eyes. Tell her the following:

> "I'm so sorry. I'm so sorry you had to go through that. You didn't do anything wrong. I love you. Please forgive me. I forgive myself. Thank you for being so brave"

4) Take a deep breath. Notice what you feel.

Again, write or create artwork about your experience. This is such a deep and easy way to clear trauma. Writing or creating artwork will help you integrate it.

If you've completed the Soul Exercises, you have
begun a process of deep healing. Reconnecting and loving
these older parts of you has the power to change your life.
If any of the exercises feel uncomfortable or incomplete,
I would encourage you to find a trusted healer or therapist
to help you work them through. Do not be afraid to ask for
assistance with this work.

Chapter 4

When Emotional Wounds Become Physical

Emotional pain isn't made up. It doesn't exist only in our heads. We experience the sting of rejection and loss in our very bodies, because our bodies and brains aren't separate. They are one unit. We don't feel heartbreak or heartache solely in our minds. Not only do we feel anxiety or depression but also the ache and pain of heartbreak and heartache in our physical bodies.

In this chapter we'll look at how our emotional pain can manifest in our bodies as physical symptoms like headaches, back pain, an upset stomach, or even chest pains. I'll reveal the three main energy centers in your body and how to listen to them more carefully. Consciously moving into your heart and body can also help release you from the mental judgments that create heart wounds. Once you understand the strength, wisdom, and intuition of your heart, you can use it to guide you into your loving energy.

Feeling Heartbreak in Your Body

When I was twenty-three years old, I had a board-licensed cardiologist diagnose me with "heart break." At the time, I had just moved home from college and left my group of good girlfriends, who had been my support system for the past four years. I moved back to Albuquerque and rented a tiny 480-square-foot apartment, sandwiched between the freeway and a cemetery. Suddenly, I went from living with six of my dearest friends and confidantes in a big house to living in a bleak white-walled apartment, where I fell asleep every night to the sound of the freeway. I was sad, I was alone, and I was depressed. It was at that time that I began to develop heart palpitations and fairly severe chest pains. I would be sleeping and suddenly I would awaken to a sharp pain in my chest that would last for about ten seconds and then subside. I lived this way for about four months until I finally went to the doctor.

After several months of chest pain and palpitations where it felt like my heart was skipping a beat, I took myself to the cardiologist. He was the most well-respected cardiologist in our city, and I remembered watching his weekly segments about heart health on the local news. I walked into the waiting room and immediately felt out of place. I was a twenty-three-year-old girl surrounded by a sea of people in their seventies. I knew that I probably didn't belong there, yet I also knew something was definitely wrong with me.

When the nurse called my name, I followed her back to the exam room. The doctor came in and did an EKG.

He looked at the results on his machine and then turned to me and said, "Tell me about your life. Have you been sad about something or stressed about something lately?"

Trying to hold back tears, I briefly told him how I had just left my best friends and moved home and no longer had any friends here. I told him I had struggled with feeling lonely.

The doctor looked at me and said, "Yes, this makes sense. Nothing is wrong with your heart. You are just suffering from heartbreak."

"What?" I asked, somewhat baffled. I was expecting to hear I had an incurable heart condition and had months to live.

"You're heartbroken," he said again, gently.

I let that sink in.

He was right. How much easier it would have been to get a pill that fixed my heart and move on. But no, I now had to deal with this revelation that I was suffering from a grave malady indeed: heartbreak.

The doctor was right. I was in an emotionally devastated state. And while I had been aware that I was sad, lonely, and vaguely depressed, it hadn't occurred to me that my maladies reached all the way into my flesh and into my organs. I hadn't realized that my sadness could extend into the very tissues of my heart and cause it to beat off-kilter. I had no idea my pain was so great that it could quite literally cause my heart to feel sharp burns.

My body *felt* the heartbreak even before my mind did. It knew what my mind could not. My body knew I needed loving and tending to. It took my heart jumping inside my chest cavity for me to really understand that my body registered this pain. Once I heard my diagnosis, I began to treat myself with radical gentleness. I would talk to my heart and let it know, "I am so sorry you are hurting right now." I began to pay closer attention to my body and listen to its requests for warm baths, hot tea, and journaling. I let myself cry and grieve the loss of my best friends. I treated my heartbreak with nurturing and compassion. In time, the chest pains completely went away.

I tell you this story to show you that heartache and heartbreak are not made up. They can be extremely physical experiences. The loss of love we feel in our lives reaches into our vulnerable and tender bodies.

Grief, longing, hurt, and loss can make their way into our very hearts themselves.

When we feel heartbroken, we feel it in our bodies.

Our Body's Energy Centers

Our bodies are more than simply bones, muscles, and tissue. They are also sophisticated transmitters of energy and information. We are living, breathing, intelligence machines. Our bodies are made of energy, and they pick up energies from their environment constantly. Have you ever felt a certain "vibe" when you walked into a room or when dealing with specific people? Is there someone who always seems to evoke a sense of peace or warmth when you are around her, or, on the contrary, have you ever interacted with someone you instinctively didn't trust? Your body knows. Your body knows when it feels danger, and it will respond by putting you on edge or creating a tension in your body. You may feel uneasy in your gut or feel your heart beating faster. When we are sensing danger around us, whether it be physical or emotional, our bodies enter fight-or-flight mode to prepare us to handle danger. Stress signals are your body's way of preparing you to take action if necessary.

It is thought in certain Eastern traditions that we actually have three main energy centers in the body. When something stressful occurs, we usually first register it in our heart or gut. People describe having a heavy tense feeling in their chest or in their gut — our bodies truly know when something is happening to us in some way. According to many of the Eastern traditions, our three main energy centers are located at the base of the stomach, in the heart, and in the center of the head. Indeed, new research is beginning to validate that these energy centers actually do exist.

When I was writing my doctoral dissertation, I stumbled upon some fascinating research from the HeartMath

Institute that revealed the incredible wisdom of the heart.[*]
They have been researching the heart and stomach for years.
In one study, researchers discovered that the heart is deeply
intuitive. They wanted to see if the heart and the stomach
could predict the future. You may have heard people say
how they predicted an event in their lives as "a gut feeling."
These researchers wanted to see if there was any validity to
the anecdotal idea that our stomach registers events from
the future before they've actually taken place, so they set
up an interesting experiment. They created a slideshow with
photographs of both neutral images and disturbing images.
The neutral images were photographs of objects, such as a
cup of coffee, a flower, a toaster, or a mountain meadow.
In contrast, the disturbing images were of events such
as a snake attacking the camera, a bad wound, or a train
accident. The researchers then hooked up participants to an
EEG, perspiration monitors, and other devices to measure
the response of both their heart and body to stress. The
participants then watched the slideshow. Their body's stress
responses were recorded and analyzed.

The results were astounding. The researchers found that
the body exhibited a stress response a full three seconds
before a disturbing image was shown. Somehow, the body
was able to predict the disturbing image three seconds

---

[*] McCraty, R., Atkinson, M., & Bradley, R. T. (2004a).
"Electrophysiological evidence of intuition: Part 1. The surprising
role of the heart. " *Journal of Alternative and Complementary
Medicine, 10*(1), 133-143.

before the participant saw the image. What's even more amazing is that the heart registered signs of distress a full five seconds before the subjects viewed the disturbing image.

Both the body and heart knew there was something scary or stressful coming. They began feeling the stress of it three and five seconds before the person consciously experienced the disturbing picture. As this study reveals, our bodies are deeply intelligent. They know things our eyes, brains, and minds can't see. There is wisdom in our bodies, especially in our heart. Our physical bodies and hearts can perceive and register information that even our conscious brains cannot. There is deep wisdom in the body and heart that often goes unnoticed. By tapping into this wisdom, we tap into a navigation system that can lead us into joy, happiness, and more ease.

Moving into Your Heart and Body
Many of us are overly stuck in the mental realm. We are moving further and further into our minds, ignoring the messages of our hearts and bodies. We are abandoning creativity in favor of mental stimulation, spending hours scrolling through social media instead of getting into our hearts and bodies and enjoying life. The problem is that being overly pulled into the mental realm will contribute to the feelings of judgment that distance us from loving.

Counteract this pull toward the mental by moving in the opposite direction. Move into your heart. Move into your body. By being in your body and enjoying all of the wonderful sensate pleasures of Earth, you begin to change your consciousness and open your heart. Instead of spending hours on social media, playing video games, or eating lunch at your desk in front of your computer, spend time painting, dancing, or cooking. Get outside and take a walk, feeling the sunlight bathe your body in light. Hug your partner or snuggle with your pet. Allow your heart to open and feel love. Notice the difference in how you feel when you make an effort to reside more in your body and heart than your mind.

Tuning into Our Heart Wisdom

The heart has a special wisdom all its own. Yet, we are often taught to disconnect from our heart's wisdom and our intuition early on in favor of more logical answers. When we have an ache in the body, we are first told to visit the doctor — not to look into ourselves. And that's okay. But science is teaching us that the heart may have a wisdom and knowledge that even scientific instruments can't touch or measure. In fact, you may be your own best healer.

The heart is the most powerful organ we have.

I had a client, Vanessa, who came to see me because of a mysterious stomach issue. Her stomach would distend and swell throughout the day and cause her tremendous discomfort and pain. Vanessa had been trying to figure out what was going on with her belly for 10 years. She had been to doctors, yoga teachers, tai chi teachers, and psychics to no avail and was currently working with a well-regarded nutritionist who sent her to me. Through all of her attempts to find healing, Vanessa had been given dozens (if not hundreds) of different supplements to take, spiritual practices to try, and diets to follow. None of them had worked, and Vanessa was tired of getting up at five o'clock in the morning to perform a spiritual practice that she hated doing. So, in our work, we took a different approach. I had Vanessa tap directly into her heart's wisdom through a meditation. Her heart spoke directly to her in meditation and told her, "Stop pushing me so hard. I need gentleness and compassion, not discipline."

With that, Vanessa changed her whole approach to healing and stopped doing the strict spiritual practice she had been given, stopped forcing herself to perform the strenuous exercise she had been told was good for her, and stopped beating herself up for not being disciplined enough. Vanessa had previously thought that in order to heal she had to push herself into stricter and stricter diets, more arduous workouts, and more rigorous spiritual practices. When we tuned directly into her heart, the advice her own heart gave her was to stop all of that and nurture herself instead.

Vanessa began to take a different path to healing, treating herself to a massage every week, sleeping in, and doing a gentle workout that felt good to her body. Soon, Vanessa was much happier and less panicked about her stomach. She began enjoying life again. Once Vanessa began this new path to healing herself, based on her heart's wisdom, her nutritionist found stomach bacteria that was contributing to Vanessa's digestive issues and they were able to formulate a diet and supplement plan that actually healed her gut. I believe that as Vanessa tuned into her own heart's wisdom first and foremost, she was able to call in the right path to healing her physical issues. She went inward first, and then her outward life was able to provide the right healing path to heal her belly.

Our Heart Strength

The heart is incredibly wise. It can perceive disturbing events, pain, and hurt easily. And it often puts up walls or blocks as protection. But, paradoxically, the heart is also immensely strong, like an ocean. The waves on top may be choppy and buffeted by the wind, but beneath the surface, the ocean is deep, still, and strong. It is peaceful, crystal clear, and protected. This is much how the heart works. On the top of our heart there may be currents and waves that are blown around by the events of life, but underneath those top layers lies a deep and lasting peace.

Plugging into that wisdom and that peace is what we are here to do. The currents of life will, at times, blow us around. But once the storm has passed, we can touch back into that deep, still place and find the strength and wisdom of the heart once again. Listen to the physical signals your body sends to help you tune into the emotional pain that you may need to resolve.

The heart is strong because it knows— no matter what— that loving will live on. Although the storms, dramas, and harsh experiences may suggest otherwise, loving cannot be destroyed. Loving is an energy that cannot *ever* be permanently destroyed. Yes, it can go into hiding temporarily, but it will not remain hidden forever. It will bubble up again when the heart feels safe. It will surface when the heart finds a way to heal.

♥

Soul Exercise #6: Getting in Touch with Your Heart

In this exercise, we will get you in touch with your heart. This may seem very subtle or obvious, but very few of us are ever taught how to connect with our hearts.

1) Make yourself comfortable.
2) Take a few deep breaths and just let go of your day and any stresses or worries you might be carrying.
3) Feel into your heart. Imagine putting your attention and energy down into the physical space of your actual heart. You can also try imagining that you are a small person exploring inside of your heart. What do you notice?
4) What emotions are there? Colors? Images? Sounds? Explore your heart.
5) Ask your heart, "Is there anything you want to say to me? Do you have any messages for me?"
6) Without censoring or judging yourself, listen for an answer.
7) If you feel called to, journal or do artwork about what you heard.

How does it feel to tap into your heart? Strange? Wonderful? Sad? This may have been the first time you've consciously tapped into your heart. Try practicing this on a daily basis and see what you notice.

Chapter 5
The Beginning of False Beliefs

As humans here on earth, transforming traumas and challenges into loving is our main task. How do we do that in the midst of so much suffering and pain? It begins with examining the false beliefs we created as a result of what we've experienced. We often create these beliefs from much younger parts of ourselves — the parts of ourselves that depended on and needed the love and protection of those around us to survive. These beliefs begin to form when we come to earth, full of open-hearted Soul energy, and then got trampled by the trials and tribulations of life.

As a natural result of experiencing hurt, our sweet beautiful heart begins to put up walls. That adorable, tender heart feels the bruises and stings of life and quite brilliantly tries to protect itself. And here is the truth — that heart of yours needed safekeeping at the time. Our brain development is incomplete, we are physically weak, and so we do the best we can to protect ourselves. There is logic to the way the heart moves. It is not irrational; it is actually deeply discerning and wise.

The problem is that we often build these walls when we are very young, not knowing that one day we will be older, wiser, and better able to protect ourselves. We don't understand that someday we will be competent, mature adults, who can navigate through life using insight and intuition. We construct walls around our hearts, not realizing that one day we will be in a position where we don't need them. We will one day be capable of protecting ourselves and able to understand when to love others and when to love ourselves. However, our young selves do not grasp this, so they do what they know how to do: erect walls and defenses to shield themselves. Despite the fact that we develop into capable, mature adults, the walls we created when we were young remain and persist.

We need to understand how we form false beliefs about ourselves in order to knock down these walls and return to a state of loving. We must eliminate our judgments so that we can remember who we are on a soul level.

How Our Brain Forms Negative Beliefs

We come into this world full of loving, and we are born into various family situations. Sometimes there is loving present; sometimes there isn't. And both are okay. No matter what extent of loving you've had in your life from friends and family, you are still capable of feeling, giving, and receiving love. You may have had a difficult childhood. No doubt there are energies to process as a result, but you are never permanently damaged. You have likely not been taught how to go back and re-do that childhood — or to re-claim the loving you were born with. But it *can* be re-claimed. That loving can live within you again, even if you've never felt it before.

If you were born into a loving and supportive family system, you have still encountered challenges in your life that may not be fully resolved. No matter what type of family you were born into, you will likely have negative beliefs and judgments that you form about yourself as a result of walking the human path.

When we endure emotionally significant events, we try to find ways to explain them. These brains of ours are data machines, constantly picking up input from the world. We are born with open minds and hearts and brains that want to make sense of our reality. As our brains grow and develop, we receive input from our life experiences and senses, and we use that input to create patterns, or understandings, for ourselves. We come in, open ourselves up, and then use what we find to make sense of the world.

One of the ways we make sense of the world is by forming beliefs. Beliefs help us categorize what we experience. The brain is the grand categorizer — it takes all the data the senses perceive and tries to form it into neat little categories. Two of its favorite categories are "good" and "bad." Our brain, whether by design or by culture, classifies much of what it experiences as good or bad. If we think about survival of the primitive man, this makes sense. We had to form snap judgments about whether the animal or human approaching was friend or foe. Or if the food we were eating was safe or unsafe. To keep ourselves alive, we had to discern harmful from safe. Our brain has a natural tendency to try to protect us, and it does an extraordinary job keeping us safe by creating instant judgments about the world around us.

Seeing Ourselves as "Good" or "Bad"

Unfortunately, our brain's ability to categorize doesn't always work in our favor. It can tend to take its categorization too far. The brain wants to understand the world—and our experience of the world—and it will place events, people, places, and things into the "good" or "bad" category. This can still be useful as we navigate the world to know what to avoid and what to embrace. We want to move toward what feels good.

So we decide, very quickly, what is "good" and what is "bad." Unfortunately, this goes for what we decide about ourselves as well. Our brains interpret everything through this good/bad lens. When we experience an event, we use the feedback of the world around us to give us information about who we are. We use other people's responses toward us to form opinions about who we really are and to form our identity, or who we believe we are.

Unfortunately, our brains are exceptional at judging ourselves as bad. When we have an experience with other people, we like to form beliefs about ourselves based on those experiences. As I'm sure you've noticed, it is often the negative experiences that have the most sticking power. Our brains tend to hold onto the negative experiences more than the positive. As small children, when we have difficult encounters with caregivers or others, we form beliefs about ourselves and our worthiness.

The problem in all of this is that we've forgotten who we really are. In our desperate attempts to define ourselves, we use our brain and its judgment of "good" and "bad" to form our identity. But who we really are isn't based on good or bad. We are based in Soul. We are based in loving. We have simply forgotten this truth.

Instead, our unconscious begins to store thoughts, or beliefs, about who we are. The unconscious is like a giant dark warehouse packed full of beliefs. Although there is no light, that doesn't mean nothing is there. Quite the opposite — a ton of information is hiding in that darkness. Beliefs that made their way into our bodies and brains are packing that warehouse. They are in the shelves and containers that line the warehouse. Our unconscious is full of beliefs, most of which we can't see. And it is these beliefs that form the foundation that guides your life.

Illuminating Our Unconscious Beliefs
Through this work, we are going to bring light into that giant warehouse. That warehouse has stored millions of beliefs, some of them useful. Others, not so much. Our

beliefs that limit our joy, happiness, and well-being need to go. And to do that, we first shine our flashlight of awareness on them. When we do, they are whisked outside into the broad light of day and we get to see them — really see them — for what they are. We get to look at where they came from, where we picked them up, and how they have affected our lives.

Beliefs are the filters through which we see the world. When we create a belief, that belief guides the rest of our lives, until is it worked through and cleared out of our unconscious. If you create a false belief at a young age, that belief will color and affect the life experiences you have as you move through life. If a small child adopts the belief "I'm not lovable" then she will see every interaction with friends, family, and future romantic partners from that lens. False beliefs create energetic walls that other people can feel. As this child walks through life, her energy field will convey to people that they should stay away, even though in the very center of her heart there exists a deep desire for intimacy and connection. Her false belief of "I am not lovable" will create a wall that will prevent her from fully receiving and expressing the loving she wants. She may even unknowingly pick partners who will leave her or abandon her, all because of the core false belief that exists in her unconscious.

Similarly, if a small child has a bad experience with a grown man at a young age, and develops the belief that "men are bad," then every experience she has with a man will be colored by that belief in some way. It will distort her reality so that in every man there is a part of him who will always be bad to her. It will be impossible for her to see the genuine good nature and open hearts most men have. She will look at all men as bad, and some part of her will always be afraid. Needless to say, this will create challenges with romantic relationships, co-workers, and work situations as she moves through life.

This process I'm leading you in is about making these beliefs conscious. It is about shedding light on the warehouse of your unconscious. We are going into that warehouse and taking some of the most important beliefs and shining our flashlight on them. Our flashlight is our awareness, our attention, and our focus. The moment we shine our awareness on these beliefs, they move from that warehouse into the big open lot out front. There, we can see them, we can work with them, and we can investigate them to see if they hold any truth. They are no longer hiding in the warehouse, affecting our lives without our even knowing.

If the thought of excavating all of your limiting or dysfunctional beliefs is overwhelming, I understand. Truth be told, you are never going to see every single belief that is in that warehouse. There are too many, and we don't need to see each and every one. If you spend your entire lifetime excavating beliefs, you still wouldn't get to all of them. I want you to focus on key beliefs that may have shaped and formed you and your life in ways that are no longer needed. These are beliefs that are in conflict with who you really are. These are beliefs that hold you back from living your authentic desires. These are beliefs that keep you in judgment of yourself and your life choices. I call them dysfunctional or false beliefs, and while they may have served a purpose for some time, if you are reading this book, your deeper truth wants more room. And to make more room for the real you, we have to bring some light to the beliefs that have been buried so deeply in that warehouse of the unconscious.

Updating Our Beliefs

Once we form a belief, the belief sticks. Even though we physically mature, the beliefs we form at a young age fail to evolve. Beliefs remain embedded in our bodies and energy fields until the now mature and wizened adult part of ourselves can go in and look at them, offer them love, and forgive them. By doing this, we update ourselves. We let go of the false beliefs our younger selves created and update ourselves with the truth, which is that we are safe, capable, and independent beings who can both give and receive love. We are no longer the dependent and vulnerable child or teen who created false beliefs out of a misunderstanding of his world.

When a younger part of us creates a belief, he doesn't realize that we will one day be a fully capable adult who can handle situations much more easily than our younger self did. Our younger wounded parts don't understand that one day we will be able to physically protect ourselves, emotionally engage ourselves in safe ways, and generally take care of ourselves and our boundaries. The younger self may have experienced terror, heartbreak, or tremendous loss. And he truly wasn't equipped to handle them. His brain was not fully formed, and he was physically dependent on his caregivers for food, shelter, and affection. He did not have a choice.

However, the person you are now, who is reading this book, is an adult. You are older, physically taller, and stronger. You have more life experience and wisdom, you've looked out for yourself and handled tough situations, and you've learned a lot. You have more freedom to take care of yourself. The current you would have been much better able to handle the situation into which the younger you was thrust. Unfortunately, it wasn't the adult "you" who was in that situation.

This process we are in is about updating ourselves and bringing ourselves current. The truth is, you are a mature and capable adult who is able to adapt to life's circumstances and keep yourself safe. You are no longer the young "you" who was abused, hurt, or mistreated in some way. You are able to take care of yourself, love yourself, comfort yourself, and give yourself all that you might need. You are longer depend on caregivers, parents, or other authority figures to get your needs met. You can meet your own needs.

And this understanding creates freedom and true loving. Knowing that you can now take care of yourself and meet your own needs means you can live life based on your authentic self. However, we can still go back and clear up any energetic residues that younger self might still have as a result of whatever it was she experienced.

The good news is that every false belief is ultimately looking to be resolved. Every false belief you may carry in your consciousness is looking for the light, looking for the truth. Every false belief is looking for its opposite true belief.

For example, that little girl who adopted a belief that "men are bad" is desperately trying to find the belief that "men can be good." She doesn't want to believe the false belief; she wants to find the truth. She is simply afraid to and, more than anything, doesn't know how. In my years of work, I have found that it is the skeptics who most fiercely want to believe. They simply don't know how. It is our nature to return to the light-filled divine essence we are. Every experience we have is ultimately trying to help us get back to that divine essence. That false belief is guiding you into finding the light that exists inside of you.

I will teach you a simple and easy way of resolving false beliefs later on in this book. I will give you the tools you need to transform false beliefs into Soul-based truth, so that you can re-pattern your reality and draw in more positive, uplifting experiences for yourself. When you change your beliefs, you change your entire reality. Until now, you haven't known how, which isn't your fault. Now you finally have the keys to undoing those false beliefs and restoring your natural flow of energy.

Recollecting Our Truth

The process of awakening is about remembering. When we look at the beliefs we've created based on our brain's faulty perception of who we are, we begin to release those perceptions. And we touch into Soul. We touch back into the essence of who we are. We touch back into the living, breathing love that is the truth of our deepest being. We release the falsehoods and negativity and allow the loving of our Soul to burst forth.

This is the truth we have forgotten: that we are living love and living light. Our brains mask that love and light when they decide that based on the events we've experienced we are somehow unworthy or "bad." Our brains simply don't understand. They think they know what they are talking about when they declare us not pretty enough, or nice enough, or successful enough, or intelligent enough. But they don't.

Your brain just doesn't have access to the truth.

The truth is you are living love. Sparkling, vibrant, gentle, always present loving. You are beyond good or bad. You are worthy. And you are loving.

Our task is one of remembering who we really are; uncovering the falsehoods and finding the gold that lies underneath. We wade past the murky waters of trauma, heartache, and loss and into the crystal-clear ocean of who we really are.

We forget who we are so that we can remember, and once we remember, we *know*. We know always and forever that who we are is blessed light, sparks of God, love embodied.

Your truth is trying to find you.

Your truth is trying to wake you up and ask if these beliefs you've formed along the way represent the highest and most real you. Your truth is desperately calling out to you: "Remember me. I am the light that shines through you. When you are bogged down with thoughts and worries about your life, I am hard to see. When you form beliefs about yourself that go against who you really are, you forget about me. But I am always here, always have been, and always will be. I am waiting for you. There is no hurry, and I know that someday we will meet again in a sweet embrace. Until then, I wait. And whisper to you in your moments of darkness that it will be okay. Sometimes you listen; sometimes you don't. But that doesn't stop me from being here. I will always be here."

This is who we truly are. We are crystal clear, shining essences who are lovable, loved, loving, and always connected to Source. We are blessed Souls, whose wondrous light is shining through us at all times. We cover up that light with false beliefs and judgments about ourselves and our lives. When we think we have messed up somehow, haven't done well enough, or aren't worthy of loving, we turn away from that light. But it beckons to us.

Spirit speaks very softly, in a whisper. You must be quiet to hear it. However, it will persist. It will always persist. It will tell you there is something more than what you are experiencing. Something better out there. It will gently remind you that there is another way to live, a way that is much more joyful, in flow, and full of living love that bursts from your heart.

♥

Soul Exercise #7: Childhood Beliefs

We are going to begin to look for beliefs that we created as a result of our childhood. We'll go deeper into these beliefs in the next few chapters.

1) Take out a pen and your journal.
2) When you think about your childhood, what beliefs did you form about yourself? What did you decide about yourself or life at an early age? What judgments did you have about yourself? Just brainstorm. Don't think too hard about this. Just list beliefs you think you may have adopted about yourself. Examples might be: I am unlovable, I am always alone, No one will ever care for me, I'm a bad girl, Nothing I ever do is good enough, I deserve to be punished for who I am. List out every single belief you can think of, even if it doesn't fully makes sense to you.
3) Keep this list. We'll come back to it.

Chapter 6

False Beliefs Create Energy Blocks

The first way we create dysfunctional beliefs about ourselves occurs through our personal history. As we grow and have various experiences, we tend to internalize those experiences negatively. Our mind is set up to create negative beliefs about who we are based on those experiences, but when we form a negative belief, we actually create a block in our energy field. Negative beliefs can be seen and felt by skilled practitioners. When I first began training in healing work, one of the exercises Robert Waterman had us perform was to place our hand about six inches from a person's body and feel for "blocks." I remember being skeptical about it until it was my turn. I used my hand to slowly scan the participant's energy field, and, sure enough, after about 15 seconds, I felt a heavy object almost prick the palm of my hand as I held it above the participant's stomach. It was not something I could make up or create in my mind. The block felt as real as the chair I am sitting in.

When we form a negative belief about our self, it actually changes our energy field. All of us have an energy field that surrounds the body. You can think of it as an energetic egg that protects us and keeps us rejuvenated with our own essential energy. Some people call this the aura. Researchers, such as Dr. Valerie Hunt, a physiological researcher at UCLA, have even begun to find scientific evidence that this energy field exists. This field of energy houses our essential energy.

Blocks are created as a result of a false belief. They feel like dark, sometimes sharp, objects in the aura or energy field surrounding the body. When we create a false belief, a block forms and the energy in the area of the block stops moving. The energy is prevented from moving. Our well-being is based on how well our energy is flowing, so when we have blocks, they affect our health and happiness.

When we are open, balanced, and free, energy moves through the energy field constantly. We feel alive, energized, and happy when we are in this balanced state. However, if we form a negative belief about our self or a negative judgment, it creates a block. The energy field is like a gentle river, bubbling and flowing along. Negative beliefs act as dams, or giant rocks, that impede the flow of that energy. When we have many blocks, our life energy is impeded. This will make us feel sad, anxious, depressed, or fearful. Our essential energy has been prevented from moving through our body. Something is wrong, yet very few of us know what it is. We've all had the experience of feeling off, sad, or angry and not knowing why. Often, what we are feeling is a block in our energy field. The natural river of our energy can't move through these blocks. It is the river that makes us feel alive, vibrant, and whole.

By identifying the false belief and bringing forgiveness to it, we dissolve the block. When I work with clients, they often come in feeling heavy, anxious, or depressed about an issue. As we work together and find the limiting beliefs and blocks and then use self-forgiveness, they report feeling light, happy, and relieved. When our energy field is moving freely, we feel light, tingly, and uninhibited. It feels like joy. Once you understand the origin of the false beliefs causing your own blocks, you can begin to clear them and reclaim your essential energy.

How Do Energy Blocks Form?

False beliefs begin to develop when we are very young and are often based on our first experiences of this world. As children, we interpret the world as being our creation. We are egocentric, meaning we cannot understand another person's perspective. Our brains have not yet developed the capacity to understand other people or that they have experiences, histories, perspectives, and desires that are all their own. All we know is our own experience, and so we make meaning based on our own feelings. Our brains are also wired to respond emotionally to the events around us. Our capacity to assess situations and experiences with logic has not yet developed. As young children then, we feel like we are the center of the world, and we have deep emotional responses to what takes place in our world. Because of our brain development at the time, we also tend to assume that everything happening around us is somehow our fault. As irrational at it may seem, young children feel responsible for what is happening in their world, even though they are not.

We internalize what we experience during this time and feel we are responsible for any perceived lack of love or care from the adults around us. Without fully developed brains, we think we are to blame if we are abandoned, neglected, abused, or unloved in any way. Young children take every experience very personally. They are trying to find their place in the world and understand who they are. They are on a quest of their identity. However, they initially base their identities on how caregivers and adults respond to them. This can be great if a child is given all of the nurturing, love, and gentleness she needs. However, being constantly attended to with love, compassion, and understanding is nearly impossible. Even small events in a child's life can be deeply impactful.

These negative beliefs can form from something as small as a harsh word spoken at the wrong moment or as large as a major trauma. I remember a time in kindergarten that affected me deeply, though it was only a small, brief encounter. My teacher, Ms. Irene, was someone I absolutely adored. She was gentle, sweet, calm, and taught us songs in French to sing at "circle time." My shy, timid, little kindergarten self absolutely loved her gentle demeanor.

One day, we were doing art projects, which was my favorite activity as a child. I was cutting doilies to glue on a piece of red paper. I only wanted a small part of the doily and so once I had cut the part I wanted, I threw the rest in the trash. I did this a few times and then heard Ms. Irene say in a raised voice, "Charmayne!!! Put the doilies in paper scraps, not the trash!" This was the first time Ms. Irene had ever spoken to me in a stern tone of voice, and I was shocked, hurt, and scared. The teacher I loved and adored, and who had been totally safe to me, had yelled at me.

Again, this was a minor incident, but as small children, our caregivers are our world. We establish our sense of inner safety on whether our caregivers feel safe. As a result of this incident, my sense of safety within that setting was disrupted. My young four-year-old brain tried to make sense of what had taken place. The only way I could understand what had happened to cause my loving teacher to yell at me was that I was wrong or bad in some way. At that very moment, my developing brain created beliefs based on the negative emotions I was feeling. Though I didn't consciously understand what beliefs were being formed, in retrospect I can see I created beliefs such as "be very careful and walk on tiptoes around people you think are safe," "creativity can get me into trouble," and "I can express myself, but not too much." These thoughts were not rational, but they manifested themselves inside of me. I felt ashamed, bad, unworthy, and scared after that incident.

Those emotions are the sign of a false belief taking root in the psyche.

Looking at the story I just shared from an adult perspective, it is evident that on that day Ms. Irene could have been exhausted, overwhelmed with a room of eighteen four-year-olds, or maybe she was particularly concerned about the environment and didn't want me to waste a scrap of paper. From my current adult self, it is clear that her raising her voice was probably not about me and wasn't a big deal. But as little kids, we are constantly trying to make sense of our world and who we are in the world. When emotional experiences occur, we make decisions and beliefs based on those experiences. My young, underdeveloped four-year-old psyche received her statements as criticism about my self-worth and creativity.

Caregivers do not always need to be perfectly safe, calm, gentle, and nurturing for us to grow up psychologically healthy. Breaks in connection, such as what occurred between Ms. Irene and me, happen. As a note to caregivers and parents who are reading this, when breaks in connection take place, you can restore connection, and false beliefs usually do not have the space to form. When there is a break in the loving, all a caregiver usually needs to do is reconnect with the child, holding her, hugging her, apologizing if need be, and letting the child know she is safe and loved. You do not have to be perfect in your life, even as a caregiver. As we are learning to do with ourselves, caregiving is about returning to love, back into connection.

That ability to do that is what makes you safe to the people in your life.

Thus, as you can see, when we are young we take what happens to us and form concepts of ourselves based on our feedback from the world. In this way, we come to know ourselves based on what other people say about us or to us and through what happens to us. This is our personal history, and for most people, their history is dotted with relationships and experiences that were less than nurturing and loving. So many of my clients have experienced very real physical, emotional, verbal, or sexual abuse.

How Negative Beliefs Form

We create a false belief when we experience an event and then use that event to create a belief that we are somehow unlovable, unworthy, or disconnected from God. Almost every belief can be reduced to a fear that we are shameful, unworthy, unlovable, unloving, or disconnected from All That Is. The truth is, we are inherently worthy, lovable, loving, and always connected to All That Is. We just don't know it.

Rachel came from a warm and loving home. She was the oldest of four children, and for three years before the first of her siblings was born, she was an only child. As a young toddler, Rachel was vivacious, full of energy, and strong. She liked to run outside, and her favorite activity was being pushed high on the swing at the playground down the street. She loved it when her father made paper

85

airplanes, and she would laugh non-stop watching them fly toward her. Her giggle was infectious, and people would do all they could to make Rachel laugh, just to hear her. Both of her parents were loving and doted on Rachel with affection, praise, and nurturing.

When she was three, Rachel's little brother was born. It was a difficult birth and her mother lost a large amount of blood during labor, necessitating several blood transfusions. As a result, her parents didn't have the same energy to give to Rachel. Both parents were stressed and preoccupied, caring for the newborn. Her mom was frail and weak for the first year of her son's life, and she spent much of her time in bed alone or with her newborn to feed and care for him. Her dad became very stressed caring for his wife and two young children. Though he tried his best to give Rachel special attention every day, she usually only received a minute or two with her father before he rushed off to heat up a bottle, go to work, or cook dinner. Rachel went from being the apple of her parent's eyes to being an afterthought, while they dealt with the pressing demands of a newborn and her mother's health.

While she always had food, shelter, and clothes to wear, Rachel felt as though she had lost what she craved most: her parent's attention. As a result, her heart began to form energetic bruises. Though she never suffered any physical abuse, she started to develop some emotional scars. Unbeknownst to Rachel, some blocks in her energy field were created in response to all this pain. She had felt so much loving . . . and then it seemed to be taken away.

In Rachel's young psyche, she formed several false beliefs as a result of losing the attention to which she had been accustomed. Straight away, her unconscious began creating beliefs about herself and the world around her. She formed several core beliefs based on the emotional trauma she experienced when her parents were no longer there for her the way they had been. Some of these beliefs included:

- Love will always leave me.
- Everyone else's needs are more important than my own.
- The world will always stop caring about me.
- I'm all alone in this world.
- I have to always take care of myself.
- I can't rely on others.
- I have to be independent to be safe.
- I'm not worthy of being adored.

Rachel formed these beliefs when her heart felt the loss of attention from her parents. At the young age of three, she adopted a belief that she needed to be self-sufficient. Her little heart was wounded when her utopia of care, attention, and loving was taken away by the demands of a newborn baby. After her brother was born and she lost the nurturing she needed and wanted, Rachel's heart closed a little bit. She began to feel the need to be self-sufficient at all costs. The loss of her parent's love was so painful she unconsciously decided it was safer simply to take care of herself. In fact, it felt safer for her to take care of not only herself, but others as well, rather than allow the loss of love and attention that she experienced as a young child.

As she grew, Rachel became increasingly independent. In the span of one year, young innocent Rachel began to feel like she had to be a responsible adult in her family. She felt she needed to help her parents, and she secretly believed that if she helped enough and was good enough, her parents would see how special she was, and they would return their attention and nurturing to her again.

At a very young age, Rachel set up a dynamic in herself based on the beliefs "If I help enough and do good enough, I will be loved." In that moment, Rachel's little body began taking on the burden of being the perfect helper. She simultaneously closed off her heart and created a hole inside herself that was desperate for the love and attention she felt she originally lost at three years old.

As Rachel grew up, the belief that she had to help enough and do good enough to receive love ruled her relationships. She became incredibly self-sufficient. In school, she was the perfect student, wanting to get good grades to show her parents how good she was and win back the love and attention she felt as if she had lost. Rachel's teachers always commented about how helpful she was — always the first to assist other students or the teachers themselves.

To feel valuable and worthy, Rachel positioned herself as a helper to her family — and later to her peers and teachers. To make sure she was needed, appreciated, and loved by her family, Rachel made herself an indispensable helper.

Rachel's parents had two more children, so life never really returned to the way it was before her siblings were born. Her mother regained much of her strength but was occupied with four children. Her father worked long hours to support the family and usually came home tired, without much energy for his children.

As Rachel grew older, she tried harder and harder to be helpful and good. When she entered adolescence and began dating, she tried to win over men with how helpful she could be to them. She revealed her strength and independence and made it clear she didn't need to be taken care of. She would bring them small treats she had made, offer to wash their dirty clothes, and even help them with their homework. Rachel positioned herself to be an independent, strong, and indispensable helper to the men she dated. Quite unconsciously, she believed that if she made herself needed enough, if she helped enough, these men would never leave her. She hoped that if she were good and helpful enough, her boyfriends would shine their attention, love, and adoration on her. She believed that to get the nurturing she needed and wanted, she would have to be the helper in the relationship. Ironically, Rachel never did allow herself to completely accept and receive her boyfriends' love and attention, even when it was given. To do so felt too unsafe and vulnerable. Thus, Rachel created an impossible pattern for herself of over-giving to win love, but because of the walls she put up as a child, she could not receive the love in her life that was given.

The men who dated Rachel experienced her as a bit standoffish. They longed to connect with the more vulnerable part of her, the part she had buried deep inside her heart. They wanted to truly know and see Rachel. While Rachel's gifts and acts of kindness were welcomed at first, her romantic partners soon started to feel as though they were being smothered. They wanted something from Rachel, and it wasn't the gifts and over-nurturing. They wanted to touch her heart and feel it. Yet, the shields Rachel constructed at three years old to cover her aching heart wouldn't allow men to get close. As a result, she experienced failed relationship after failed relationship. The intimacy and connection that she deeply longed for always seemed to evade her.

The false beliefs Rachel created at three years old remained with her through adulthood. Though deep inside she longed for love, affection, and intimacy, these false beliefs prevented her from ever finding the love she so desperately craved. Instead of feeling safe enough inside herself to allow herself to be vulnerable and connect with a romantic partner, Rachel closed herself off from experiencing real love. She decided that safety was never having to rely on another. And so, Rachel became very independent, self-sufficient, and a good caretaker of others.

As you can see, Rachel formed beliefs about herself and love based on a very early experience of perceived loss of love as a child. At the young age of three, she began to form beliefs that a loss of love or attention was her fault, and that to win back that love, she needed to give, help, and perform. Rachel compensated for a perceived lack of worth by over-giving and over-nurturing. However, because these actions came from a compensation and not an authentic place of expressing her love, her actions fell flat. The loving and attention that Rachel so craved always eluded her. She had not found her own wholeness, and so every relationship was destined to fail.

Life is set up for us to find our wholeness, our worthiness. Every failed relationship and experience is established to encourage us to eventually look inward for our worth and loving. This is not a worth that is dependent on how much you give, how well you perform, how much weight you lose, or how much money you make. This is a worth that is based on the divinity that exists inside of you. There is no way to be unworthy; it is impossible. You are born divine, as is everyone else on the planet. You can never lose your divine worth. It is only possible to forget our inherent connection to God and forget that we are worthy.

Every time we feel disappointed, abandoned, or rejected, life is moving us closer to finding the inner loving and worthiness that is our buried treasure. Even the false beliefs that Rachel formed were never wrong because they eventually helped point her back to discovering her self-worth. Her entire life was in service to directing her toward finding a sense of inner loving for herself. No part of her life was ever wrong. It was all part of her journey to uncover her wholeness.

Rachel came to see me when she was 32 years old, after a long string of failed relationships. As we worked together to find the false beliefs she created and to learn to love and accept the young part of her that had felt abandoned by her parents, Rachel's life transformed. Her chronic anxiety eased. Her sense of heaviness, depression, and malaise cleared. Rachel began to feel lighter, happier, and more vital. Over the course of our work together, I noticed that her face changed from being taut and pinched to being open, relaxed, and soft. She went from looking like she was 38 years old to looking like she was still in her twenties. By undoing and clearing the false beliefs, Rachel returned to her true essence, which was a gorgeous and sweet being who was ready and able to give love and receive it in return.

About a year after she first came to see me, Rachel began online dating. At 33, she met Eric, a kind, sweet man who loved to shower her with love, small gifts, and adoration. Instead of defaulting to her typical over-giving behavior, Rachel allowed herself to receive his love because she knew, deep down, that she was worthy of being loved like this. Rachel had found a sense of self-worth that allowed her to receive. In return, she responded with deep appreciation and authentic loving, which delighted Eric and enabled them to form an intimate bond based on both of them being their true selves.

Rachel and Eric were married a year and a half later.

You Can Return to Wholeness

The good news is that you are still whole. It may not feel like it, but you are. Underneath the holes and wounds that living life has created in your psyche is a whole being. Understanding that the wounds and hurts were never really about you will help you return back to your wholeness. There is light in your life and on your path, no matter the darkness from which you've emerged. Our task is to rediscover that light. And whether your childhood was good or bad, whether you repeatedly suffered a broken heart as you grew up, it doesn't matter. The light can shine through all of it.

Your personal history is going to provide you with a wonderful way to return to loving. So far in your life, you've lived with a certain set of beliefs. You've operated within a system. You can think of your life as a big spider web — everything is connected to everything else. When one part of your life begins to change, it affects the rest of the spider web. When you start to identify and shift false beliefs, your whole system will change. Your energy field changes, and thus your body and mind change as well. When you use self-forgiveness to dissolve the blocks in the aura and energy field, your energy and vibrancy fill you again. It will feel like returning to your essence (or discovering it for the first time).

Your Soul has a great plan for you. Your Soul has orchestrated all of this. Your Soul has known you would be born, experience hard events, become hypnotized by all the false beliefs and expectations around you, and lose your connection to It. And it's okay. Your Soul also wants something very grand for you. It wants you to wake up. It wants you to see and know your real truth. This is such a special moment in life, when we answer the call of the Soul. It is the moment you start living life for you, rather than for everyone around you.

♥

Soul Exercise #8: Clearing Out False Personal Beliefs

Awareness begins to shift patterns. The moment we become aware of the unconscious beliefs we have created, they begin to unravel. We will now bring more awareness to the false beliefs you adopted growing up. This can be the most difficult part of this work. Often, false beliefs are buried so deeply within our unconscious that they can be hard to see. I encourage you to trust whatever you feel or notice. Let yourself notice whatever pops up in your thoughts, without censoring yourself.

The beliefs you may feel you have may not make any logical sense. In fact, I can guarantee that many of them won't. Remember it is often a younger, more irrational version of ourselves that created these beliefs. As you do this work, allow whatever beliefs that want to pop into your head to appear. Don't censor them or try to make sense of them. Allow whatever wants to arise, to arise. This is so important. You want the beliefs stuck in your unconscious to surface. Don't use your logical mind to fight beliefs that want to emerge because they don't make sense. Just allow those beliefs to show themselves; give them some space and air to breathe.

To begin, we are going to explore an event in your past that was never fully resolved. When a difficult life event isn't fully processed or integrated, we will find ourselves being pulled back to the incident. We will think about it frequently, returning to the event while stuck in traffic or drifting off to sleep. The event, though in the past, won't seem to leave us alone. This is a sign that a part of your energy remains stuck in that event.

First, let's start with a little preparation. Take out a pen and some paper. Find somewhere quiet to work. Make yourself comfortable and take a few big, deep breaths. You can say a little prayer or call on any spiritual support that feels good to you. Take a few more big, deep breaths, feeling your breath move into your lower belly and into your legs and feet. Allow your breath to gently and easily fill your body, breathing all the way into your feet and toes.

(continued on next page)

After a couple minutes of breathing, ask God/Spirit/the Universe to show you an event or two from your past that needs resolving. Notice what you see or feel. Don't censor it or judge it. Just write it down. When you've finished writing, take a few big, deep breaths. If it feels too intense to do this alone, find a therapist or healer you trust to help guide you through this.

Pick one of the events you just saw. It could be when you were called names in school or when a family member hurt you in some way. Pick a memorable event you still haven't forgotten. We tend to forget events, or the charge around them fades away, once we've worked through them. Pick an event you still find yourself thinking about, perhaps starting with a smaller one as you familiarize yourself with this process. Think about the event and how you felt. Remember, *you are not in that event.* It is in the past. You are an adult now and *never have to live that scenario again.* If it helps, imagine the event playing on a television or movie screen. You are not in the event; you are simply observing it.

Write down every thought or belief that you can think of in response to these questions:

1) What did you decide about yourself after that experience?
2) What did you decide about life?
3) What did you decide about God?
4) What beliefs did you form about yourself as a result of that experience?
5) How did you judge yourself after that experience?

These are the judgments and beliefs you formed because of this event. Keep this list; we are going to return to it in Chapter 9, where I will teach you how to dissolve and clear these beliefs in a matter of seconds. You may have only a few sentences, or you may have pages and pages of beliefs and judgments. Trust whatever comes forth. We will clear all of these beliefs in a matter of minutes later on.

Again, if this process is intense, please reach out to a therapist or healer as soon as you can. You can reference the final pages of this book for a list of NFT practitioners who specialize in this work or go to my website at www.charmaynekilcup.com for more resources.

If you feel antsy to start clearing these beliefs, you can skip to Chapter 9. If you want to find more beliefs you might have unknowingly picked up from the culture around you, keep reading.

Chapter 7

Identifying Mass Consciousness Beliefs

Another way we pick up dysfunctional beliefs is through "mass consciousness." I use this term to embody the beliefs, views, and moral code the majority of a culture holds. Mass consciousness dictates our societal "norms." Each culture has its unique ideas about what makes a successful human. Very rarely do these beliefs reflect the truth, which is that you were wonderful and perfect from the moment you were born. And you still are. Your unique expression of God is already blessedly and truly worthy, as are you. There is nothing you need to change about yourself to be worthy and lovable. You arrived on Earth already a success. But again, we forget this truth. And instead we absorb messages that are drilled into us at an early age about how we "should" be — to be of value, to be wanted, to be loved, and to be desired.

In the last chapter we explored how our own personal false beliefs develop based on events in our childhood, which then cause energy blocks that hinder our connection to Soul and unconditional love. Unfortunately, our culture also contributes its own set of false beliefs, interfering with our ability to recognize our true worth. Mass consciousness beliefs shape our feelings about body image, financial success, and even sexuality. They begin to influence us the moment we are born, especially as they relate to gender identity. They have a powerful impact on our lives, pressuring us to want to "fit in." In this chapter we will examine which mass consciousness beliefs you hold that are unsupportive; and then eliminate those beliefs that don't serve you. When you begin to feel restless in your life, it is a sign your true self wants to reawaken and shed these mass consciousness beliefs, and the shame surrounding them, in order to reconnect to the joy of the Divine love that awaits you.

Common Mass Consciousness Beliefs

Mass consciousness beliefs tell us either consciously or unconsciously how we should look, how we should act, what we should do with our time, and what our relationships should look like. You know you've stumbled upon a mass consciousness belief when you hear a voice in your head telling you that you "should" be something other than who you are. These are the unconscious and conscious rules to live by that were impressed into us from the day we were born. Some examples of our culture's mass consciousness beliefs include:

- Education and hard work are the only keys to success.
- If you are female, your duty is to get married and have children.
- If you are male, your duty is to be ambitious and make lots of money.
- When you find a mate, it should be someone of the opposite sex and of the same cultural background.
- If you are female, you should marry someone from a similar class or from a higher financial bracket.
- You should get married between ages 22 and 30.
- You should have 2.5 children after you get married.
- You should work, save money, and then retire.
- Successful means making lots of money.
- Academic degrees make you worthy.
- You should always look young, beautiful, and thin, in order to be worthy of love.
- Your weight determines how lovable and worthy you are.
- All women should want to be mothers.
- Making lots of money is what makes you valuable.
- Having a prestigious job makes you worthy.
- Being Caucasian is what makes you worthy.
- Success is based on how well you do in your career.

- If you have money but didn't work for it, you don't really deserve it.
- Pursuing creative endeavors will never lead to success.

These are examples of the social "norms" in Western society, specifically in the United States. This is the script society subconsciously hammers into us from the day we are born. Other societies will have different norms, or ways that life "should" unfold. If you deviate from that specific path, you will begin to wonder if something is wrong with you, or if you made a wrong choice somewhere along the way. This is the power of mass consciousness. It can make us second-guess everything about who we are and the choices we are making. It is what causes us to compare ourselves to other people, who we mistakenly believe to be more "successful" than we are, simply because they have acquired the trappings in life that our culture's mass consciousness has deemed worthy or important.

Mass Consciousness and Body Image

How many of us spend hours, days, and even years fighting against ourselves? Our bodies are one of the primary places into which mass consciousness has lodged itself. If you live in Western culture, I can guarantee you've spent vast amounts of time worrying about if your body is pretty enough or handsome enough, thin enough, toned enough, blonde enough, blue-eyed enough, white enough, tall enough, short enough, and on and on. There is such a narrow view of what makes an attractive body in our culture that if you are born with any part of your body that doesn't fit the norm, you will unconsciously feel as if something is wrong with you. That you aren't "normal." That you aren't "enough" or beautiful or worthy. You will somehow feel that you don't fit in, and you will receive the message it is your fault and that you should feel ashamed.

Who says your body isn't okay? Really think about it. Who has decided that your body is good or bad, beautiful or ugly? Who made up what a "good" body is? Really think about it.

What gives people — any people — the authority to declare what a "good" or "bad" body is? Truly. If you believe the shape, size, or color of your body isn't good enough in some way, it isn't your fault. Society's programming enters us the moment we are born (or even before). While we are in utero, we are already unconsciously picking up messages about who we are, what our gender means, and what our skin color signifies. This programming is so thick and potent and powerful that it can even make us somehow believe we aren't worthy. The reality is, none of it is true.

If you feel anything negative about your body, it isn't your fault. To base our perceived worthiness on how we look is a distortion and dysfunction in the culture, not in you. This is a cultural problem, not a personal one. Please do not feel you need to change yourself, alter yourself, or adjust yourself to fit the cultural distortions. Each and every person on this Earth is completely and inherently worthy, just by the very nature that they exist. By living the truth of who you are, you become a spiritual rebel. You refuse to allow the cultural message that you are not good enough to distort your sense of self. It takes courage and bravery to love yourself and accept yourself in a culture that bombards you with messages that you shouldn't. We are told every day we should hate our skin tone, our cellulite, our extra weight, our not-enough weight, and so on. To accept and love yourself just as you are is counter-cultural and takes immense bravery. The spiritual truth is that every shape, size, and skin tone is equally worthy and equally deserving of love and acceptance. You are worthy of love and acceptance in this moment just the way you are.

Mass Consciousness and the Quest for Success

Another place mass consciousness seems to lodge itself is in what it means to be successful. We are told early on that to be successful we need to attend school, excel in school, and then pursue a career that will eventually support our retirement. Often, material success is valued over passion, service, creativity, and heart fulfillment. Women receive contradictory messages about success, because mass consciousness is changing its views on women's roles. This leads to confusing messages that women should strive for the top and be successful but also be wonderful mothers who can nurture children and take care of the household duties. All at the same time.

In the United States and many other countries, success is often defined as financial. You are successful if you make lots of money and have a prestigious job, big house, nice car, and boat you take out on the weekends. However, success does not have one definition. The reality is that success is different for every person and is based on his or her own particular soul mission and authentic desires. True success for you might mean having a job you want to go to every day, having a circle of friends who support you and value you, having a small home to call your own, having a relationship you love, or having a family of your own. Maybe success for you is the ability to make art every day or to have time to meditate. Success for you could be rescuing an animal from a shelter and giving it a good home. What success is for you truly depends on who you are and your own unique make-up. There is no one type of success; there are only myriad versions tailored to your particular needs, desires, and soul missions in this lifetime.

Mass Consciousness and Sexuality
Another strong mass consciousness hypnosis has to do with religion. In Western countries, there are heavy overlays stemming from Judeo-Christian culture. Many of the clients I work with have an internalized idea that they are sinners; that they are worthless and need to prove themselves to God. These beliefs seem to strongly take root in our

concepts of our sexuality. Almost all of my clients who have grown up in religious households have had deeply embedded beliefs about their sexuality. Christian/Catholic culture has created the belief that sexuality is wrong, dirty, or shameful if experienced anywhere outside a married heterosexual partnership. Young children who experience sexual urges (as is natural and as we are biologically wired to do) will often begin to judge their sexuality at a young age, if it isn't normalized by loving and caring caregivers. For most young children, displays of sexuality are met with condemnation and judgment from the world around them. This creates a deep-rooted shame that causes many of my adult clients to struggle.

So many forms of sexuality are judged in our culture. Sexual urges and desires at a young age are shamed. Sexual desire for a same-sex partner is considered wrong or shameful. Wanting to be a different gender is considered wrong. Touching yourself in pleasurable ways is considered dirty or a sin.

This is all a grand distortion.

And yet it is so pervasive that I have many clients who cannot openly and lovingly experience their sexuality, even in a church-sanctioned partnership. If we shut down one part of our sexuality, we shut down all of it. Sexuality was meant to be an open, playful, creative, and sacred energy. When we judge our sexuality in any way, we judge life-force energy that was originally meant to connect us back to God.

Sexuality originated as a gift from God. It is a potent force that when used consciously can expand your loving and expand your consciousness. It was never meant to be considered dirty or shameful. Religion and a patriarchal structure have corrupted this beautiful sacred energy in many ways.

Women in particular seem to suffer from this distortion of sexual energy. Christianity believes Eve brought suffering and sin to the world. Whether we realize it consciously or not, women are blamed for the sin of sexuality. I work with many women who have experienced sexual abuse, and what I find in almost every single one is a belief the abuse they experienced was somehow their fault. Women who have been victim to sexual abuse often believe they deserved it somehow or that they are "dirty" in some way as a result of it. This is the result of a strong cultural overlay that blames women for the corruption in the world. Women have historically been (and still are) blamed for men's domination of them.

This creates a deep sense of shame and worthlessness in women, especially those who have experienced sexual abuse. They know what happened to them was wrong, but they usually internalize that wrongness as their responsibility. They tend to form beliefs that they are bad, wrong, or shameful. Instead of seeing the *situation* as wrong, they see *themselves* as wrong. This is part of the distortion of sexual energy that blames the feminine and makes it responsible for the wrongdoing in the world.

106

As I mentioned in Chapter 2, when I was studying to be a therapist, one of my professors said, "The victim takes on the shame of the perpetrator." I find this to be especially true in sexual abuse. The way our society is set up, the victim of sexual abuse is often the one who internalizes the shame of that event. The victim will feel as though he or she did something wrong, when nothing was actually ever his or her fault.

I've had many clients who felt they did something wrong when they were sexually abused as children, because they enjoyed the pleasurable sensations in their bodies, even though they sensed something was amiss. However, even small children who feel pleasure when they are sexually abused are not doing anything wrong. They are responding the way their bodies are designed to respond. Our young bodies are meant to respond to pleasure. That response isn't shameful or wrong in any way. Unfortunately, the context in which they are experiencing pleasure is not set up in a healthy way. Children who experience sexual abuse are victim to a situation that does not support their authentic sexual expression or power. But the experience of feeling pleasure is never wrong. Our sexuality is never wrong. We are often in situations that are more about domination than authentic sexual expression, but this doesn't make us or our sexuality wrong in any way — and never has. It makes domination instead of loving wrong. But it doesn't make *you* wrong. Or your sexuality. Or your heart.

107

No matter what might have happened to you, you were never wrong. Nothing you did was wrong. Your sexuality is a gorgeous and beautiful aspect of you that should never have been dominated, condemned, judged, or used. If your sexuality was violated in some way, I am deeply sorry. It never should have happened and it wasn't your fault.

Mass Consciousness Instruction Begins Early
Our programming about what it means to be *normal* begins with our very first breath. For example, the moment we are conceived, we start acquiring subliminal messages about what it means to be male, female, attractive, successful, and "normal." In other words, from day one we start picking up messages from our surroundings about what it takes in our culture to be worthy. Our most potent desire is to know we are worthy and loved. Mass consciousness tells us there are certain ways we are worthy. The truth is, our worthiness already exists within us. It isn't something we have to find or prove. Our worth is embedded into our Souls the way our cells are embedded into our physical bodies. We cannot be separate from our worth. We can only forget that we came in already worthy.

When we forget our worth, we go in search of it. We look for the path to worthiness, and our culture is quick to tell us what that path is. If you are a woman, the path to worthiness is to be beautiful, slim, nice, easy-going, people-pleasing, sweet, sexual, Caucasian, and heterosexual. Women are expected to find a man to marry; settle down with him; and then become a mother. Beauty, marriage, and motherhood are how we define success for women. For men, that path to worthiness is to be athletic, smart, tall, Caucasian, ambitious, strong, and wealthy. This is what we see as a successful, and thus worthy, man. So much of our mass consciousness beliefs are based on how we determine worth as a man or as a woman. The truth is, *none of it is true*.

The Influence of Gender Identity

From their very first days on earth, little babies are treated differently and given different objects based on their sex — that is, if they are born male or female. Typically, babies who are female are wrapped up in pink blankets and clothes while boys are dressed in blue. From the moment a baby's sex is known, it is being unconsciously programmed with information about what it means to be male or female. Female children are taught to wear soft colors, play nicely, learn how to listen and relate to others, and are given babies as toys to practice their mothering. Male children are encouraged to be a bit more wild, adventurous, loud, and action-oriented. They are given swords, trucks, and superheroes to play with.

While hormonal differences between males and females do create some very real natural differences in behavior, culture has in many ways locked both genders into those set patterns of behavior. Girls and boys are given different prescriptions for what it means to be a girl or boy. Women are rewarded and praised for "normal" female behaviors, such as feeling, relating, empathizing, gentleness, and nurturing. Men are rewarded and praised for "normal" male behaviors such as taking action, conquering, and illustrating drive and ambition. And while none of those actions is bad, we get into trouble psychologically when only the parts of us that match our social conditioning are rewarded. If we deviate from the rules of what it means to be male or female, then we will likely feel shame about it. We may feel that we aren't man enough (strong, capable, ambitious, successful) or aren't a perfect woman (beautiful, a good mother, attractive, nice). And this can be a tremendous source of shame for people. This is the power of mass consciousness beliefs—they have the ability to cause us to internalize a sense of shame. When part of us doesn't naturally align with the culture, we will feel shame about that part.

Adam grew up in a small Midwestern town, where boys were taught to be men, and girls were taught to be women. When Adam was a young boy, his Dad enrolled him in baseball. He himself had played baseball and insisted that every son he had would also play baseball. So, at the age of five, Adam joined Little League. And he enjoyed it. He loved hitting the ball, running as fast he could, and sliding in the dirt. He loved the smell of the field and playing with his friends. With his family's support, Adam continued playing baseball through his teen years and became one of the best players in his town.

At the age of 10, Adam was in practice when an event shifted his life and sense of himself. He was playing second base when one of his teammates ran into him so hard that he fell, twisted his ankle, and broke his foot. Immediately after it happened, his coach ran onto the field where Adam lay and helped him to his feet. He asked Adam if he was okay. Not wanting to cry in front of his friends, Adam said "yes." At the tender age of 10, he already knew somehow that if he cried from the immense pain in his foot, his teammates may not respond kindly.

As Adam tried to walk, he felt sharp shooting pains in his foot and ankle. He called the coach over and told him that his foot really hurt. He could feel the hot stab of tears threatening to erupt from behind his eyes. All he wanted at that moment was for his mom to come over, hold him, and take care of his foot. Instead, his coach yelled from across the field, "Be a man, Adam. Walk it off." With his teammates watching his every move, Adam knew he had to do everything he could to push back the tears that he so desperately wanted to release. So he walked on his broken foot for a couple of days, insisting it was fine when his parents asked about it. Finally, his mother forced him to go to the doctor, and he was put in a cast. He felt proud of that cast, as if his foot was proof that he had been to battle.

In those few moments when Adam laid on the baseball field in intense pain and in the few days after, he formed many beliefs, some of which were:

- Being a man means I should never cry.
- Being a man means to always be strong.
- Being a man means you walk it off.
- Being a man means you avoid looking weak.
- I have to be strong at all times, so no one makes fun of me.

In the instant his coach responded to his injury, Adam swallowed his tears and formed many beliefs about how he needed to be if he was going to be a man. In doing so, he began to close off his heart to anything that felt like weakness. And because his coach had inadvertently told Adam not to acknowledge it, he pushed down his pain. He had to shut down all of his feelings, in order to ignore his pain. And so, Adam had to shut down his heart. To hide the pain that threatened to make others perceive him as weak, Adam buried his feelings deep inside and put big iron doors with a lock over them. He walled off his own heart. In the process, the young, innocent, fun-loving Adam got buried and pushed down with it. The sweet, young Adam got locked up that day when Adam told himself to "man up" and be strong because of the mass consciousness messages about gender.

After that, Adam stopped having as much fun playing baseball. He was still one of the town's best players, but he began taking the game more seriously. He became team captain, and when one of his teammates was injured or hurt, Adam was the first to encourage him with a "walk it off" or "be strong." Adam had shut down his feeling with so much force and thought he was doing the right thing to "be a man." His beliefs then influenced the rest of his team, and soon there was a group of young men who felt more comfortable ridiculing each other when they failed than offering compassion.

As Adam grew, he dated many women. At age 29, he married Stephanie. Stephanie absolutely adored Adam, but she often felt like he didn't express his love for her. She was constantly trying to get him to talk about his feelings. Each time she did, he grew silent, his jaw tightened, and he would go pour himself a scotch and turn on the TV. Frustrated that her repeated attempts for connection went unmet, Stephanie became even more emotional and, eventually, hysterical, trying to break Adam out of the deep freeze in which he seemed to be stuck. Her attempts to rescue that young wonderful Adam she sensed was deep inside of him never worked. By the end of their marriage, both of them felt disappointed, bitter, and resentful of each other, and they divorced in their late thirties.

As we can see from Adam's example, his wounding occurred when he received cultural messages about what it was to be a man. To be anything other than a "man" was shameful and to be avoided at all costs. Unfortunately, Adam was so indoctrinated about "manhood" that he shut himself down, as that is what the men around him did and told him to do. In doing so, Adam emotionally disconnected from the world around him.

To "be a man," Adam disconnected himself from his heart. Yet in doing so, he also disconnected from his ability to feel joy, playfulness, connection, beauty, and wonder.

Think about early messages you received about what it means to be a man or woman. What are the implicit rules drilled into you as you were growing up?

Wanting to Fit In

Our social programming begins the day we are born and only deepens as we get older. As we grow, social norms are constantly being reinforced by the world around us. We see them in books, movies, and stories, and we hear them from friends and family who tell us how we *should* live our lives. Often, another person's "should" is actually a reflection of their mass consciousness beliefs about what is right and good and moral, ideas that were likely programmed into them. If you ever think to yourself that you *should* pursue a certain path, you are most likely stumbling on a mass consciousness belief. Our true nature has only desires and curiosities, but never "shoulds." Our Soul only craves experience; it doesn't express judgments about what we should or should not do. Mass consciousness beliefs leave little room for creativity and authentic expression.

Mass consciousness beliefs restrict authentic expression, restrict spontaneity, and restrict joy. They are all about getting us to fit in. And there is this silent unconscious threat that if we don't fit in, we will die. This threat can be extremely powerful. Our most basic need and desire is to fit in, to have a tribe, to feel belonging, and to be safe in a family or community. If some part of who we are is in opposition to what mass consciousness says is normal, then it triggers that part of us that is absolutely terrified of being an outsider. And if some part of us doesn't fit in, we worry that we won't be loved and that we won't be safe.

Ask yourself right now, if you don't fit in, will you die? Just ask yourself. To the primitive parts of our brains, not fitting in makes us think and feel we are in extreme danger. The primitive brain is wired to keep us safe at all times. It doesn't care what you feel or what you logically know about a situation. It only knows if there is danger and if you should fight, flee, or freeze. Anything that threatens your safety within a community will feel terrifying and you will automatically find yourself avoiding it at all costs. Mass consciousness beliefs carry so much weight because they trigger our most basic instinct: to stay with the tribe and be safe. They hit us where it really counts — our desire and need to fit in and be loved and accepted.

Finding Freedom from Unsupportive Mass Consciousness Beliefs

Mass consciousness beliefs are a powerful force. It is nearly impossible to examine and disassemble all of your mass consciousness beliefs; there are so many and they are so influential. However, we are going to examine the ones affecting your life the most. Our goal is to see if we can find more freedom for you. We want to give you the option of either subscribing or not subscribing to mass consciousness. I want you to feel you have the power to opt out of a belief that isn't true for you. This doesn't mean we are doing away with all mass consciousness beliefs; it is impossible to do so. In addition, you don't have to get rid of all of those beliefs before you can be yourself. Our goal is to see which mass consciousness beliefs serve your true self and which ring false for you.

Some mass consciousness beliefs may not pose problems for you; they may actually support you. For example, I loved school and was quite good at it. The mass consciousness belief that education is important and that you should receive as much as possible aligned with my natural desires. My dream of pursuing my education was naturally supported by mass consciousness, which was expressed through support from family, friends, and even strangers who heard the news that I was planning to obtain an MA and PhD and congratulated me. They encouraged my decision, told me I was doing the right thing, and would ask me how school was going. I was even treated to a fancy dinner after my graduation. I was socially rewarded for this choice. There was no need for me to *not* get educated, simply to prove my separation and independence from mass consciousness. We don't have to fight mass consciousness solely for the sake of fighting it. Sometimes, it can actually be supportive. Education was in the flow of my personality and my life, so I was able to pursue that desire without much protest or conflict. I allowed myself to be supported by mass consciousness beliefs that were naturally in line with who I am. I didn't need my education to make me feel whole or worthy in some way, and so I was able to simply receive that support with an open heart.

However, I've had other parts of who I am that were in opposition to mass consciousness beliefs, such as my career choice, my body, and my marital status; therefore I have had to work through them to gain more freedom from them. We need to explore those beliefs that challenge our inner sense of our own worth. These are the beliefs that are dysfunctional and cause damage to our psyche. These are the beliefs we've either inherited or created as a result of our personal wounding, and these are the beliefs we need to clear for our own personal liberation and for that of our children. With regard to other parts of myself, I have had to consciously resist what mass consciousness was telling me. For example, my body has never been one that fits mass consciousness's depiction of the perfect female body. From an early age, I started to become aware that my body should be a certain way. I remember as early as second grade feeling like, somehow, my body was not right. I was plump, short, and had unruly dark hair. The girls who were considered popular seemed to smile a lot and were all skinny, blonde, and had long ponytails. I remember from this early age clearly feeling as if there were something wrong with me.

No one was telling me I was too short or too chubby. Okay, maybe a few mean boys made fun of me. But no one told me that I should be petite, blonde, and blue-eyed, yet I somehow felt I should be.

Where did that come from?

When I was growing up, I played with Barbies, all of which were tall, slender with teeny tiny waists, Caucasian, blonde, and blue-eyed. The experience of playing with Barbie's alone contributed to the mass consciousness beliefs I developed and adopted. Not to mention the heroines and "beautiful" women in books, movies, and TV shows, who were usually some version of a Barbie — thin, blonde, Caucasian, and blue-eyed (again, another function of mass consciousness at work). I was born brunette, brown-eyed, and have always tended to be heavier than most of my peers. In this way, my physical appearance was in direct contrast to what mass consciousness deemed acceptable. This caused me tremendous anguish as I was growing up, because I so desperately wanted to be thought of as pretty, attractive, and desirable.

What I looked like was so in contrast with what mass consciousness told me I *should* look like that I developed anorexia in an attempt to fit in. I felt tremendous shame about the fact that my body was different, and in my head my body wasn't acceptable. I had severe anxiety and starved myself for ten years just to try to achieve the image I thought I had to embody to be seen as attractive. In this way, mass consciousness did not support my natural self. It was directly at odds with who I am and caused me tremendous suffering. To heal, I finally had to pull myself out of mass consciousness, look at my own unique form of beauty (which we all have), and appreciate who I was naturally, instead of trying to fit in. I had to find support from myself and within myself to be who I am and eliminate mass consciousness beliefs. I had to let go of the culture and society validating me and instead find validation within myself.

In this way, mass consciousness beliefs are not necessarily "bad" or "good." They are either supportive or unsupportive. Our goal is to challenge mass consciousness beliefs that suggest that some part of us is bad, wrong, ugly, worthless, or shameful. We want to find freedom from the mass consciousness beliefs that are unsupportive to our true selves.

We all have parts of us that contradict the culture or are countercultural. As described, one of mine has been my body, and the other is my career choice. To be self-employed as a healer goes directly against the culture that tells me to find stability, security, and a dependable job. To be spiritual, conscious, and in touch with yourself is also countercultural. We live in a society that celebrates the superficial. To be a person like you or me — who is dedicated to finding our authentic selves, living from our hearts, and finding our true spiritual selves — is to be countercultural. And that's okay! I support you in being who you truly are. I support you in finding the "you" that exists beneath all the rubble and baggage of society. I support you in finding your true voice, your true identity, and your true desires.

My mother describes mass consciousness as a pot full of crabs. You have probably heard of this analogy before: When one crab tries to escape, climb up that wall, and out of the pot, the other crabs will just pull it back down into the pot. Mass consciousness is that energy that wants to pull you back down into the crab pot. It is the psychic force in our society that wants to keep homeostasis and preserve the status quo. It wants, more than anything, to preserve and promote "normal." Do you know that feeling of being pulled back down into the pot? You may have been told you were too smart, too stupid, too fat, too ugly, too pretty, too successful, or too much of a failure. Anytime you've received a message that you weren't "enough" in some way, that is mass consciousness trying to pull you backdown into the pot. Anytime you've heard you weren't enough, or weren't good enough, it wasn't the truth. It was mass consciousness and people's personal wounding trying to get you back into that pot, with them. You *can* escape that pot and embrace your true self and love her unconditionally.

Reawakening from the Haze of Mass Consciousness
What are some of the mass consciousness beliefs you've adopted? It is impossible not to be influenced by mass consciousness in some way. You can think of mass consciousness beliefs as a green ooze that starts to coat you the minute you're born. Mass consciousness has an

energy so thick and so powerful it is like a heavy haze. And when you are born, you are immediately covered in that haze. Some people are able to resist the haze better than other people. It doesn't have to do with how good or how wonderful they are. Some bodies and energy fields are simply better at resisting the haze of mass consciousness.

Those beliefs about ourselves and how we "should" be, we tend to pick up almost by osmosis. For me, that haze of mass consciousness was so thick it somehow invaded my body and young psyche early on. It didn't come from TV or media, as my siblings and I weren't allowed to partake in either. But somehow, I picked up on this cultural ethos that who I was as a person was not okay in some major ways. I learned somehow that there was a "right" way to be, and I believed I was badly failing at it.

So, what happens when we are "hazed" by mass consciousness? We usually live our lives the way we are "supposed" to or expected to by society. We grow up, get married, have 2.5 kids and the white picket fence, and we raise children, work, and retire. Again, there is nothing wrong with this life. Absolutely nothing. The only issue occurs when and if we start to wake up to a deeper yearning for more and find ourselves feeling suffocated by this particular life. Our souls may wake us up to our missions in this lifetime, and we may realize that what we thought we wanted isn't what fulfills us at all. Many people hit adulthood, having done everything the right way, and still feel a sense of chronic dissatisfaction.

It may present as depression, anxiety, or a malaise. It may emerge as an illness, or accident, but many people begin to feel a yearning deep inside themselves. They start to yearn for *more*. Sometimes they know what that "more" is. Sometimes they don't. But deep inside, an explorer starts to re-awaken. Deep inside, that young wonder-child begins knocking from within the depths where she has been buried. She starts tapping from the innermost recesses of the heart and calls out, begging for attention. The true self begins to emerge.

Some people ignore the call. They may feel the wonder-child call, but they look away. Usually, the call grows stronger, so it may take more energy to resist it. A person may numb the call with drugs, alcohol, medications, TV, social media, or shopping. The part of her that wants to maintain the status quo resists the call. The result is usually greater anxiety and depression. But for those who answer the call, an awakening occurs.

Once they answer the door to the wonder-child knocking on the other side, life begins to change. If you are reading this book, you have answered the call. This book is about waking up to your real self. If you made the decision to read this book, know that you have answered the call. You've made the brave and courageous move of stepping out of your comfort zone into an exploration of the heart and your true desires.

So, what happens when we answer the call of the wonder-child? For a while, life might get messy. We've constructed ourselves around our beliefs, many of them false. To step forward into a more fulfilling life based on connection with our true self, we have to examine those beliefs and deconstruct the ones that no longer serve our wholeness and happiness.

♥

Soul Exercise #9: What Beliefs about Gender do you Hold?

We are going to explore some of the mass consciousness beliefs that have had an impact on you. We'll start with some of the most powerful and basic beliefs that are programmed into us, beliefs about masculinity and femininity. Get out a piece of paper. I want you to create two columns. On one column write "Men are...." and on the other column write "Women are..." Now, describe what you believe men are and women are or should be. List any and all beliefs that come to mind. What do television shows and movies tell you about what it is to be a man or woman? How are successful men portrayed in the media? And women? Who did you want to be like growing up and why? Which qualities did you try and emulate? What did family or caregivers tell you either implicitly or explicitly about what it means to be a man or woman? Were you expected to keep the peace and not speak your mind when you were a young girl? Or were you taught not to cry or show emotion when you were a young boy? Were you taught not to date outside your race or culture? What masculine or feminine behaviors were you rewarded for and punished for? List all of them.

Our aim is to bring these beliefs out from their hiding places into our unconscious so we can give them room to breathe. Once we can see them, we can keep the beliefs that support us and clear the ones that don't. In every culture, there are dysfunctional mass consciousness beliefs that instill a sense of shame and lack of self-worth in people. These are the beliefs we want to examine. These are the beliefs that need consideration. We want to look at the beliefs that are working against you and deconstruct them. You'll know you are fighting a mass consciousness belief if you find yourself feeling bad about who you are or any of your life choices.

♥

Soul Exercise #10: What are your Personal Mass Consciousness Beliefs?

Now that you've had some practice at this, think about other ways you have felt unworthy in the culture you grew up in. Was there anything about your appearance, your career choice (or lack thereof), your relationships, or your desires, that were judged by the external culture? In what ways were you ridiculed, teased, or told your choices were "bad?" Again, make a list of the places where who you were didn't fit in with who you were told to be.

After you've completed these exercises, keep your list. I will teach you the process for deconstructing and clearing these beliefs in just a few pages.

Finding Your *True* Beliefs

Again, it's okay to have mass conscious beliefs. Nothing is *wrong*. The only question is, "Do those beliefs continue to serve you?" Do they uplift you and bring you more into your own loving? Or do they bring you down into shame and comparison? If they create a sense of shame, guilt, or unworthiness within you, they are beliefs that are not true for you. Beliefs that are true will make you feel lighter, freer, and more energized.

Walk toward that which uplifts you and brings you joy. That is the path of loving. The Universe completely and totally honors every choice you've ever made. And yet, Spirit also wants *you* to know what an incredible and lovely being you are. Are you ready to let go of the beliefs that keep you stuck, trapped, and in various degrees of self-loathing? Those beliefs are not true. Beliefs that are true will make you feel worthy, connected to yourself, vibrant, free, and alive.

As you start to challenge your mass consciousness beliefs, it doesn't mean that the loving you have with families, friends, and partners disappears. By clearing out your false and dysfunctional beliefs, you start to tap into your own loving. And when we start to tap into our own loving and stop needing others to love and accept us before we can feel okay, our relationships often blossom into an even greater depth of loving. If they don't, trust that it is the highest good for you at that moment. As we grow deeper into the truth of who we really are, we don't need external validation in the same way we did before. We unplug from needing our family, friends, culture, and authority figures to validate us. We validate ourselves, and in doing so, we unleash a torrent of loving for both ourselves and others. We learn what unconditional love truly means. This tends to deepen our relationships as we learn to accept ourselves and others completely.

Learning to plug into your own loving will create only more loving in your life, not less.

Chapter 8

When Personal Beliefs and Mass Consciousness Collide

As explained in the last couple of chapters, we develop two different types of beliefs as we grow up. We form our personal beliefs, which are unique to us and our own history. These are the beliefs that solidify as the result of specific experiences and relationships. In addition, we have mass consciousness beliefs, which are the beliefs society and culture program into us from day one about what it means to be worthy. These are the "shoulds" we somehow adopt, as if by osmosis. They are often heavily influenced by moral codes that are passed down from generation to generation.

Beliefs become even more complicated when mass consciousness beliefs and false personal beliefs collide. When you layer mass consciousness beliefs onto your personal history, you encounter a mess. You receive confused messages about how you aren't good enough, or attractive enough, or successful enough because of things you did or because of who you are.

This is a lie.

The task of the self-forgiveness work I teach is to go back and undo those negative dysfunctional beliefs that you picked up both through the course of your personal history and through society's messages. When we do this work, we reclaim our energy from those times and places where we were taught that we weren't good enough, strong enough, wise enough, intelligent enough, beautiful enough, and all the other "enoughs" that are programmed into us.

Please hear this: *You are already enough.* There is nothing you need to do, nothing you need to alter, to be worthy. You are already enough. And if you don't believe me, that's okay. You don't have to believe it for it to be true. You don't have to feel like you are enough to actually *be* enough. Hopefully, we can help you begin to know and understand your enough-ness.

When Mass Consciousness Beliefs Compound Personal Beliefs

Ginger was a client of mine who demonstrates what happens when mass consciousness beliefs and personal beliefs intersect. Growing up, Ginger was a sweet young woman. She dearly loved animals and spent her early years rescuing injured birds and rabbits that she stumbled upon at her family's 20-acre ranch in Wyoming. Ginger was also a beautiful young woman. At an early age, she began puberty and developed breasts at 11 years old. The boys at school began taking notice of shy, young Ginger. She didn't pay too much attention to them and kept focused on her studies and care-taking of animals.

When Ginger was 15 years old, she began dating Mike, a popular and handsome boy who went to her school. He played sports year-round and was generally liked by his peers. Mike had noticed the beautiful Ginger and had begun pursuing her with flowers and charming little songs he would sing to her across campus. Ginger, though shy, felt special to have Mike's attention. Other girls at school craved attention from Mike and dressed provocatively to receive it. Ginger was flattered that he even took notice of her.

Soon, they began dating. As teenagers are meant to do, they began exploring their sexuality. Ginger was slightly afraid of sex and wanted to keep their after-hours antics relegated to kissing. She told Mike she wasn't comfortable with anything more than kissing. However, every time they made out, Mike would try to put his hand somewhere on her body. Ginger would move it off. After three months of this, one night at the end of a date, Mike put his hand on Ginger's shoulder and pinned her down in the car. He kissed her hard, harder than he ever had before. He began to put his hands on her breasts, and Ginger tried to move them away but couldn't. As he began moving his hands downward, Ginger got increasingly scared. Normally Mike would back off the minute she moved his hands away, but this time he wouldn't let her.

Sensing an increasing panic as Mike's hand started to aggressively fumble underneath her panties, Ginger screamed. At that, Mike, who was a bit stunned by his usually quiet girlfriend's scream, backed off. He removed his hands and sat back up in his seat. Ginger opened the car door and walked inside to her family's home, without looking back at Mike or saying good-bye.

She walked straight to her room and began to cry. After that incident, Ginger formed some beliefs about herself, including:

- My sexuality gets me into trouble.
- My sexuality is powerful.
- My sexuality is dangerous.
- This is all my fault.
- Men want my body more than anything else about me.
- Men aren't safe.
- I can't be alone with a man.
- Men cannot be trusted when it comes to sex.
- I'm safe if I stay away from men.
- Something about me is bad, if this is what happens to me.
- All men are dangerous.
- My body isn't safe.

She created these personal beliefs as a result of the specific trauma she experienced. Quite unconsciously, Ginger began blaming herself and her sexuality for what had occurred in the car with Mike. She had this sense that something bad had happened to her and it was somehow her fault. She believed *she* was the problem, rather than the event itself. Ginger began to carry a sense of shame about herself. She felt dirty somehow, like she wanted to clean the very insides of her body out, but couldn't.

After that event, Ginger's whole demeanor changed. She went from a bright, sensitive young woman who enjoyed time with her family and few close friends to always wanting to be alone. She preferred solitude more than anything else and would spend her free time in her room. Her body even began to change. She began to look as if she were caving in on herself. Ginger's chest took on a sunken look, and it appeared as though she might just crumple into a little ball.

After this incident, Ginger, who had always attended regular church services, began to throw herself into church even more. She started going to the local bible study every Thursday night and reading her bible in the morning before school and at night before bed. Church was the one place where Ginger felt safe. She felt that if she followed the rules, God would protect her. She felt she could redeem herself.

Unfortunately, in her extremely conservative Christian church, the messages she received only reinforced her beliefs. As a result of her intensive religious studies, Ginger formed more beliefs about herself, including:

- Women are the root of evil.
- Women must cover their bodies to keep men from their uncontrollable sexual urges.
- Sex is shameful.
- Women who have sex are shameful.
- I am full of sin.
- I am shameful.
- I've betrayed God by engaging in sexual acts.
- God needs to punish me.

These mass consciousness beliefs only compounded Ginger's original trauma. Out of fear, she walked straight into a religious community that had strict rules about sexuality. Ginger thought if she followed the rules, she would be saved and wiped clean of what had happened to her in the front seat of Mike's car. However, the rules in which she found safety were also what exacerbated her feelings of shame. She found both conscious and unconscious messages that what had happened was her fault and that she should have prevented it.

Ginger grew up, and while other girls in her town went off to college, she remained home and looked after her family's farm. Though her heart yearned to know and feel romantic love with another, Ginger never allowed herself to open up to a relationship again. She lived with her parents until her old age, contenting herself with a safe life in her family home. As a result of this experience, which scared Ginger so deeply, she gave up on her dreams. She gave up on the life she wanted as a little girl and instead retreated to the safety of conservative culture with its many rules.

As you can see, the messages Ginger received from her religion, family, and culture compounded the sense of shame and personal false beliefs that resulted from a traumatic incident in her boyfriend's car. Shame was met with more shame. Ideally, when we feel shame about ourselves in some way, it would be met with loving, acceptance, and grace. Shame only survives when it hides. If we speak about our shame with people who can love us unconditionally, it dissolves. However, when we speak of our shame with people who only use it to shame us more, it drives the shame deeper into hiding and deeper into our bodies.

I had another client, Donna, who struggled with the collision of mass consciousness beliefs and personal beliefs. Donna was a 47-year-old homosexual woman of African-American descent. She grew up in Arizona and was one of five African-American people in her entire high school. Her earliest memories centered on feeling like an outsider. Her family was Mormon, and though she somewhat felt like she belonged in her family, a part of Donna was always aware that she didn't quite fit in. The Mormon religion she grew up in looked down on homosexuality, and Donna remembered receiving shameful messages from a very early age about her sexuality.

Donna came to me because she felt depressed and frustrated that she couldn't seem to find any sense of happiness in her life. At 47, she was a successful corporate executive in Chicago, but she couldn't shake this feeling of heaviness in her chest and stomach. She described it as depression, and it felt like a grey weight that prevented her from enjoying anything good in her life. She was well off financially, but she yearned for a relationship and to feel a sense of happiness in her life.

In our work together, we sought to find the origin of this grey, heavy feeling Donna carried with her. In a guided meditation, I had Donna ask when she first felt this feeling and she responded, "I was three years old." I asked Donna what had happened around three years old, and she said she started pre-school and remembered walking in and the other kids staring at her. She was the only African-American student in her class, and for the first time in her life she really felt like she was different.

Her time in pre-school wasn't easy. The other students ostracized Donna and called her names. She was rarely asked to play by the other children, and her teacher never once intervened to help her feel included. Donna was able to make one friend, Jessica, who approached her during her first week of pre-school and asked her to play dress up. Donna and Jessica have been close friends since that day.

While working with me, Donna had another significant memory surface. She remembered being 11 years old, and she knew at that point that she was attracted to girls more than boys. She wanted to tell her parents about who she was but knew that she couldn't. Growing up in the Mormon community, she instinctively knew it wasn't safe to share this part of herself. So, Donna kept her desires a secret. She eventually confided in Jessica, who accepted her completely. In her current life, Donna largely kept her sexual identity private.

Donna had experienced trauma around being a minority in both her ethnic identity and sexuality. She was bullied for being African-American in a largely Caucasian and Hispanic community, and she also felt an instinctive shame around her sexual orientation, which was compounded by the Mormon church in which she grew up. Over and over, Donna experienced being told in both implicit and explicit ways that she was wrong. She was told she was wrong for looking different and feeling different from the people around her. She received overt messages from her church that who she was attracted to was wrong. She also received negative messages from the culture around her when she was called racist terms, ignored in stores, and served last in restaurants. From that experience, Donna internalized certain core beliefs about herself, including:

- It isn't safe to be who I am.
- Who I am is wrong.

- God punishes those who are different.
- I must fit in to be safe.
- Having darker skin makes me less valuable.
- There is something inherently wrong with me.
- It is wrong to be angry.
- I am worthless.

Donna had both personal wounding and mass consciousness wounding when she was bullied as a young child for being African-American. She then had mass consciousness shaming around both her race and her sexuality because she grew up in a culture that placed higher value on lighter skin and heterosexual preferences. In response, Donna had a hard time finding any sense of self-esteem or self-worth. There were very few people or organizations around her that could mirror back to her that she was beautiful, worthy, and that her desires were right. Donna was shamed for who she was instead of supported. And so, she shut down. She became guarded and quiet and carried a deep anger about the unjustness of her situation that she was careful never to express.

In our work together, I helped Donna clear the false beliefs that she adopted in response to her upbringing, using the technique you are about to learn. We also went back and talked to Donna's young inner wonder-child and let her know that was valuable, lovable, and completely worthy, even if the culture around her didn't recognize that. After doing that work, Donna seemed happier, more easily able to laugh, and her heart felt more open. She began smiling and felt comfortable speaking her mind at work. She soon received a promotion and, best of all, was able to form some true friendships with her colleagues. Eventually, Donna even started online dating, and last I spoke to her, she was enjoying meeting new people and warming up to the idea of a long-term relationship.

♥

Soul Exercise #11: How Do the Groups You Belong to Make You Feel?

Take a survey of the people and organizations around you. Write down all of the organizations, friend groups, clubs, and religious groups you are part of. They can be formal groups or simply the people you hang out with. Ask yourself the following questions:

- Do these groups help dissolve your shame or intensify it?
- Do they support your most true self, or condemn it?
- Which people and groups nourish you?
- When you are interacting with these groups, do you feel lightness and expansion, or a feeling of contraction and heaviness?

♥

Soul Exercise #12: Which of Your Personal False Beliefs Were Compounded by Mass Consciousness Beliefs?

Think back to a time when you had an experience that was personally painful or challenging. Did the groups you or your family were part of support you or shame you for what you went through? Were you afraid to disclose what had happened to you out of fear of being ridiculed or shamed? If you were part of a religious or spiritual group, was that a positive experience for you or a negative one, or both?

What would have been helpful for you at that time? What kind of nurturing, support, and words of comfort would have been good for you to hear? Close your eyes and imagine going back in time and saying those words to your younger self who needed to hear them.

Notice what happens in your body as you do this. You can journal about this experience or even write a letter to your younger self.

Find Those Who Can Help You Heal

The world would have us believe that we are unworthy, deeply shameful, and inadequate in almost every area of our lives. This is a false belief. You are breaking free of the false beliefs from your own personal history and that the culture has instilled in you. You are finding the truth — that you are magnificent. You are completely and totally worthy as you are. You are gorgeous. You deserve all the good stuff life has to offer: the loving relationships, an abundance of money, work that you enjoy, health, inhabiting and owning your body. You are learning that life doesn't have to be all suffering, all work with no gain. Life is here to be enjoyed.

Your body is here to be felt and cared for. Relationships are here to be loving support. Work is here to be inspiring. Abundance is your birthright. You are already a success just because you exist. You are deserving of so much good. This is the truth.

As we begin to explore the false beliefs we've created based on personal events in our lives and the culture at large, it can feel very isolating at first. So many people let false beliefs run their lives and it can feel like you are a stranger in a strange world when you begin to dissolve your own false beliefs. You might look around at the grocery store, or at school, or even at your own family and think, "Why do people insist upon keeping their suffering?" Once you are able to drop much of the suffering caused by false beliefs, it might feel baffling to watch people defend their own limiting beliefs. That's okay. They will wake up to the truth of who they are when they are ready. In a strange way, much of the world is having fun playing with their own false beliefs. If no experience is "good" or "bad," then playing with false beliefs is just as useful an experience as dissolving false beliefs and living with joy. It is all a matter of what you choose. What do you *want* to experience?

When you are first learning about shame, it is important to find people you can trust to meet you with loving and non-judgment. This may be friends, family, a therapist, or a healer. Find people who you can trust with the precious, most vulnerable parts of yourself. Actively search for groups and friends who support your true self.

So often the false beliefs that develop from our personal experiences become heightened by the mass consciousness beliefs that surround us every day. This can make it especially hard to break free from the beliefs that leave us feeling unworthy, inadequate, or unloved. Finding your tribe or a support system can make a huge difference in your ability overcome shame, forgive yourself, and heal.

Are you ready to learn one of the most powerful healing techniques that exist? Keep reading. . . .

Chapter 9
Healing with the Power of Self-Forgiveness

So now you've seen how beliefs form and have identified some of the core beliefs that have been unconsciously running you. Our next step is to transform those false beliefs and uncover the joy and loving that has been held hostage inside of you. Buried within each false belief is a pocket of loving and worthiness. When we unpack the false belief, those gorgeous energies of loving and worthiness are released and can flow through our bodies and energy fields. This is the beginning of us living from our true selves.

The antidote to false beliefs is self-forgiveness. To heal ourselves, all we have to do is forgive ourselves for all the ways we believed we did something wrong or believed we *were* wrong. You never actually did anything wrong or were wrong. Truly. You experienced life, in its grand fullness. You experienced the good, the bad, and the ugly. It is all part of this grand journey called being human, and there is no grand being in the sky punishing you for anything you did. There is no judgment from God or from your Soul. There is only experience and learning. So we use self-forgiveness to remind us of this. We use self-forgiveness to help return us to our sparkly, light-filled essence.

Self-forgiveness is the medicine we use to heal ourselves. In his book, *Forgive for Good*, leading forgiveness expert Dr. Fred Luskin writes that:[*]

- Forgiveness is for you, not the offender.
- Forgiveness is taking back your power.
- Forgiveness is about taking responsibility for how you feel.
- Forgiveness is about your healing and not about the people who hurt you.
- Forgiveness is a trainable skill.
- Forgiveness helps you get control over your feelings.
- Forgiveness can improve your mental and physical health.
- Forgiveness is becoming a hero instead of a victim.
- Everyone can learn to forgive.
- Forgiveness is not condoning unkindness.
- Forgiveness is not forgetting that something painful happened.
- Forgiveness is not excusing poor behavior.

---

[*] Luskin, Fred. *Forgive for Good: A Proven Prescription for Health and Happiness*. New York: HarperSanFrancisco, 2003.

- Forgiveness is not denying or minimizing your hurt.
- Forgiveness does not mean reconciling with the offender.

You can see that forgiveness is an experience that benefits you. It is solely for *you*. You forgive yourself to create freedom from what others have done to you. You forgive yourself to create freedom from any ways you have judged what you have done to others. Using self-forgiveness is a way of taking your power and energy back from a situation that might have hurt you. This is about forgiving you, *for you*.

Forgiveness is the best gift you can give yourself. It is the best medicine I have found to heal trauma, relationship issues, anxiety, and sadness. Forgiveness creates true healing. It is how you move from being a victim to being empowered.

You are worthy of forgiving yourself. No matter what you have experienced or what you have done, you are worthy of forgiveness. There might be a small voice in your head that says you are not worthy of this, but you are. *No matter what has happened*, you are still worthy.

The Healing Power of Self-Forgiveness

You didn't do anything wrong. Not ever. You were *never* wrong. Your heart was never wrong; your loving was never wrong; your soul was never wrong. Who you are has never once been wrong. It may not feel that way, but it is the truth.

143

Even if you were told differently or believed differently, *who you are* has never once been wrong.

Self-forgiveness is the most powerful method of healing I've ever discovered. It is the missing link in therapy and healing modalities, which are often focused on "fixing" the person or putting him or her back together so he or she can feel normal again. Self-forgiveness is an entirely different approach that creates true and lasting healing. With self-forgiveness, we come to understand that we never did anything wrong; we just didn't understand our lives or understand God. Self-forgiveness is the panacea for the Soul. It is not a Band-Aid, but a true healer. It is a vital and essential step for healing.

Self-forgiveness heals the Soul.

When we forgive ourselves, we put ourselves back into alignment. You'll experience it as a deep peace that washes over the body. It isn't something we try to mentally think through or convince ourselves of. It is a deep experience of release and coming back home. When you forgive yourself, you return to grace.

Again, in the history of your life, in the history of your Soul, you've never truly done anything wrong. For the Soul, there is only experience. And yet, being the human beings that we are, we judge our experiences. Our minds are set up to judge. They are set up to see "good" and "bad" — it is how we have survived for so long. If we can categorize and label, we know what is friend and what is foe. There is nothing even wrong with how the mind labels everything as good or bad, nothing wrong with it at all. Yet, after a certain point, it stops serving us. We start craving more peace in our life. We get tired of our judgmental mind.

Self-forgiveness is the way to lasting healing. It is the secret ingredient you have probably been missing in your life. Self-forgiveness, above everything, is about finding a sense of freedom or peace inside yourself. It is about releasing the self-blame, disappointment, sadness, shame, anger, and resentment that occur as a result of growing up in a world that often doesn't see or support who we really are. When we forgive, we magnetize back our power and energy from all of the people and places who might have taken it. We reclaim ourselves. We harness our power, energy, and loving. We fall back into a state of grace.

I want to be clear: I am not talking about forgiveness of others. Forgiving others is a different topic for a different day. I will tell you this: *Forgiving others isn't nearly as important as forgiving yourself.* We've got it backward in that we think we need to forgive others before we can feel peace. Nope. I'm going to make a bold statement here: Forgiving others doesn't matter. Forgiving yourself does. We need to forgive ourselves, and then we feel peace. We then often naturally wind up forgiving others, but it isn't an effort and it is nothing we need to strive to do. Forgiveness of others happens quite easily *after* we forgive ourselves. It starts with you. When it comes to healing, other people don't matter — you do. Self-forgiveness is the most important work you can do. It frequently clears up places where we have been angry, hurt, or resentful of others. Doing the self-forgiveness work brings you back into a state of loving. And that is your true home.

Releasing Self-Judgment

Self-forgiveness takes us out of self-judgment and drops us into loving, which is our natural state. When we are in a state of loving, we are aligned with the truth. When we are in fear or self-judgment, we become anxious or depressed, which is our false state. It is an unnatural state. Our loving is who we really are, which is why it feels so good.

I'm going to teach you the modality I use with clients. I have found this technique to be absolutely life-changing. It is simple, but don't let that fool you. It is profound. You'll feel for yourself just how powerful it can be.

The technique I want to show you, I learned from my teacher, Dr. Robert Waterman. When I experienced self-forgiveness myself for the first time, it was while working with him. I had worked with therapists before for my own personal healing, which had been immensely useful for me. However, once I sat in front of Robert Waterman and he had me say one of the forgiveness statements that I am now going to teach you, my life changed. In that very moment, I felt as though a soft and gentle world opened up inside me. Before that, my mind and psyche had felt a bit harsh. I was harsh with myself and disciplined myself in all ways possible. I watched what I ate, I exercised five times a week, I said the right things to family and friends, and I

criticized myself when I said stupid things or was clumsy.
I spent a lot of time and energy making sure I did things
the "right" way. When I worked with Robert and I said one
little forgiveness statement, I felt flooded by this warmth.
My mind went quiet. I felt peace — for the first time I could
ever remember. I didn't have the ten voices in my head,
telling me I wasn't good enough and that I needed to go for
a run after class and make sure I cooked a healthy meal for
dinner. I didn't have the inner rules or the inner dialogue,
telling me to stay on track. I simply felt this blissful moment
of peace and connection. Since then, I've had a level of
peace and love inside that doesn't ever go away. Even in
times of stress or chaos, there is a deep peace that stays
with me.

It was in that moment working with Dr. Waterman that I
knew I had stumbled upon something absolutely magical. It
was in that moment that I became passionate about teaching
this incredible healing therapy to others.

And so now I teach you. I am going to guide you in
the process I learned to clear false beliefs. Engaging in this
process takes us out of dysfunction and back into loving.
And that loving, that warm yummy feeling of loving, is
what God feels like. When you return to that loving, it feels
like coming home. It *is* home.

CHARMAYNE KILCUP

♥

Soul Exercise #13: Learning How to Forgive Yourself

So how do we forgive ourselves? Take out the list of beliefs you created in the exercises in Chapters 5, 6, 7, and 8. You should have a list of personal beliefs and a list of mass consciousness beliefs. Personal beliefs are the ones you formed from events in your life, and mass consciousness beliefs are those you picked up from the culture around you about what it means to be worthy. Look at both of your lists. Scan them for the belief or cluster of beliefs that feels most alive for you right now. Which one or ones call out to you for a little healing right now?

1) Start with one belief. Use this phrase in front of your belief: "**I forgive myself for judging myself for believing** _____." For example, a belief I carried for most of my life was that my worth was based on how I look. When I do this forgiveness statement, I put the words I gave you in front of the belief and get the following phrase: "I forgive myself for judging myself for believing that my worth is based on how I look." Be sure to incorporate the exact forgiveness phrase. It is important to use the self-forgiveness phrase just as I listed it. The way it is composed reminds the psyche that the belief itself was never wrong, just like we never did anything wrong. The only issue arises when we judge ourselves for having had that belief. The issue isn't the belief itself. It is how we've judged ourselves for having it. So, make sure you use the phrase "**I forgive myself for judging myself for believing . . .**" This phrase is the key to undoing blocks in your body and energy field.

2) Go ahead and write the whole belief statement and forgiveness statement out with your selected belief. You won't always need to write it out, but just to familiarize yourself with the process and embed it in your memory, write it out now.

3) I want you to say your forgiveness statement aloud. Then take a deep breath. Notice what you feel.

(continued on next page)

148

4) Take a pause.
5) What do you notice in your body? Just notice. Scan your body for any new sensations or feelings that arise.
6) Go ahead and make your way down your list of beliefs. Put the forgiveness phrase "I forgive myself for judging myself for believing _____" in front of each phrase. Say it aloud. Take a deep breath. Notice what happens.

The deep breath after every forgiveness statement is very important. Don't overlook that step. It allows the mind to quiet for a moment and the forgiveness statement to enter into the body and clear itself from your cells. Don't forget to take that deep breath.

That's it. The whole process is so incredibly easy. Find the belief, place the forgiveness statement in front of it, say it aloud, and take a deep breath. Notice what it feels like for you after doing the forgiveness statements. If you aren't feeling a shift in your body, you may have to adjust the wording in the belief. The forgiveness statement coupled with the belief is the magic here. Each statement is like a key that unlocks the blocks in your energy field. Sometimes it can take a few variations on the belief to find the exact right key. After finding the right phrase, my clients usually report feeling clearer and lighter. It is usually easier to breathe. If you don't feel those things, there may be another belief in there that needs some attention. Go deeper. What is the belief that really wants to be cleared right now?

One by one, move down your list of beliefs and use the forgiveness statement to clear them. Notice how you feel.

Here are some examples of forgiveness statements:

o I forgive myself for judging myself for believing that I did something wrong.
o I forgive myself for judging myself for believing that spiritual people shouldn't have money.
o I forgive myself for judging myself for believing that women shouldn't be leaders.

(continued on next page)

- I forgive myself for judging myself for believing that I did something wrong.
- I forgive myself for judging myself for believing that what happened was my fault.
- I forgive myself for judging myself for believing that I deserve to be punished.
- I forgive myself for judging myself for believing I've let God down.
- I forgive myself for judging myself for believing that I'm shameful.
- I forgive myself for judging myself for believing that who I am is wrong.
- I forgive myself for judging myself for believing that I am unlovable.
- I forgive myself for judging myself for believing that men should never be vulnerable.

How Forgiveness Statements Helped Estelle Heal Her Anxiety

Estelle was a 45-year-old divorced mother of two who came to me because she knew instinctively that something inside of her needed healing, but she wasn't sure what it was. She said that on a day-to-day level, she felt anxious, afraid, and sad most of the time but she couldn't figure out why. She knew her divorce had been traumatic, but she acknowledged that even before then, she had always carried a sense of anxiety. She said that for as long as she could remember, it felt like there was a terrified voice in her brain that followed her every move, trying to get to get her to think of the 1,000 things that could go wrong in every moment. At times, Estelle said she felt almost paralyzed by anxiety.

I could see right away that Estelle was a deeply warm and caring person and an excellent mother. When we spoke on the phone, I could feel the love in her heart emanating from her energy field, but it felt like it got blocked at a certain point and couldn't fully move through her body or outward to other people. I could sense that Estelle was a deeply sensitive individual with genuine concern for those around her. Yet, she found herself struggling with anxiety more than feeling a sense of connection to the people around her.

I have found that when I see clients who are deeply sensitive and also prone to anxiety or depression there is some kind of event or relationship in their history that disrupted their ability to freely give and receive loving. I work with many clients who are like Estelle in that they are empathic, compassionate, and want to love themselves but have a hard time figuring out how. In every case I have worked with, there was some kind of trauma that diverted their energy from their heart center up into the mind. And when we leave our hearts and go into our minds to try to stay safe, we get stuck in anxiety.

To begin helping her heal, I asked Estelle what it was like for her growing up. At once, Estelle's voice began to waver and she explained to me that she had a difficult childhood. Her mother was kind and loving toward her and her two siblings, but she was also quiet and submissive. Her father was an alcoholic who worked in construction. Every day after work, he would come home, pour himself a tumbler of whiskey, and sit in front of the television. After about two hours, he would be called to dinner by Estelle's mother, and the family of five would sit down to dinner. And the nightly hell would begin.

At dinner, Estelle's father, Joseph, would begin his nightly taunting of his family. He would pick on his wife and accuse her of being too skinny and weak to really satisfy a man. He would criticize the dinner she had cooked, occasionally even throwing his plate of food when he found the meal to be particularly unsatisfactory. And then he would turn on the children. He would tell Estelle's oldest brother that he was ugly, stupid, and incapable of making his own way in the world. He would tell Estelle's other brother that he was lazy and fat. And he would tell

Estelle, the youngest, that she looked like a scared field mouse and that she was weak, just like her mother, and that she would never find a man who would want her. These nightly dinner-time taunts happened every night, except for weekends when the parents would go out with their friends and come home after the kids were already in their rooms, pretending to be asleep. Estelle lived in terror when her father was home. Even when he wasn't, she was always hypervigilant, unsure as to when he would be home and if he would be drunk.

As Estelle and her brothers grew, the nightly taunts would escalate. When they were teenagers, Joe began to feel his physical power over his children diminish and so increased the abuse. He began randomly hitting the children after dinner. The oldest brother would try to protect the younger two by taunting his Dad so that he would be hit instead of them. Though her eldest brother received the worst of the physical abuse, Estelle felt terror every waking minute she was home. She felt sad and guilty to watch her brother be beaten nearly every night. She felt ashamed that she couldn't protect him, her other brother, or her mother. She felt completely and totally powerless.

To cope, Estelle began spending as much time as she could out of the house. She would stay in the library after school and complete all of her homework. When she was home, she would spend time in her room, studying as a distraction and reading books to escape. Her home felt uneasy and full of threats. She never knew when her dad would be home, and she never knew when she was next in line for a verbal or physical beating.

At age 18, Estelle received a scholarship to a college in Ohio. She left immediately and made it a point to rarely return home. Now, as an adult, she has been home to visit her mother and will occasionally visit her father who now has Alzheimer's and lives in a nursing home.

Though her father is no longer a physical threat to Estelle, the years of constant abuse have taken their toll. Living in a state of perpetual terror the way Estelle and her mother and siblings did greatly affects a person's nervous system. Because of the continual trauma, Estelle never got to let down her guard. She developed a hypervigilance so that even when she was safely in her house watching television at night, a part of her always felt terrified. Something inside of her was always scanning her environment for the next place of danger or source of abuse. Because of this, Estelle's nerves were fried, and this created the habitual sense of high anxiety.

Estelle needed help healing. To begin, I had her close her eyes and visualize calling forth her childhood self. I had Estelle look at the six-year-old version of herself, who was subject to her father's nightly taunts. I had her really look at this young part of herself and notice what she was feeling and what she was wearing. And then, I had Estelle talk to that inner six-year-old and say, "I'm so sorry. I am so sorry you had to experience that. You didn't deserve that. You didn't do anything wrong. I love you. Please forgive me. I forgive myself." At that point, Estelle began to cry. I encouraged her to feel all that she was feeling and allow it to move through her body. Estelle said she felt such a sense of love for that little girl, and she felt sad for all that she had to endure. We worked more with this inner little girl, and at the end Estelle said she felt a sense of peace that she had never felt before. She said her body felt lighter and freer than she had ever remembered.

When I tuned into Estelle, her energy field had changed immensely. Before this process, her energy field felt tight, contracted, and heavy. After this meditation, I could feel her heart begin to heal and soften. Her energy started to move downward, away from her head and toward her heart. Estelle began to occupy her body once again. She began to feel a sense of peace.

In our subsequent sessions, Estelle and I uncovered the beliefs she unconsciously created as a result of the abuse she experienced. I could see that some of the beliefs that Estelle unconsciously picked up were:

- I have to be perfect to be loved.
- Nothing I do will ever be good enough.
- Love is abuse.
- Love is painful.
- I'm unworthy of unconditional love.
- Women have to be quiet to be safe.
- Men cannot ever be trusted.
- I have to hide to be safe.

- It is impossible to be safe.
- I deserve all of the bad things that have happened to me.

After finding some of these beliefs, I had Estelle use forgiveness statements to clear them. One by one, I had her say each belief with a forgiveness statement in front of them:

- I forgive myself for judging myself for believing that I have to be perfect to be loved.
- I forgive myself for judging myself for believing that nothing I do will ever be good enough.
- I forgive myself for judging myself for believing that love is abuse.
- I forgive myself for judging myself for believing that love is painful.
- I forgive myself for judging myself for believing that I'm unworthy of unconditional love.
- I forgive myself for judging myself for believing that women have to be quiet to be safe.
- I forgive myself for judging myself for believing that men can never be trusted.
- I forgive myself for judging myself for believing that I have to hide to be safe.
- I forgive myself for judging myself for believing that it is impossible to be safe.
- I forgive myself for judging myself for believing that I deserve all of the bad things that have happened to me.

- After each statement, I had her take a deep breath. One by one, the beliefs dissolved. Estelle reported feeling lighter and clearer after each forgiveness statement. When we finished, Estelle's energy field had completely changed. I could feel a sense of golden amber-colored light flooding her energy field. Her energy continued to move down from her head and into her body. Her heart opened and I could feel it receiving and giving loving.

Estelle had made peace with her loving. From the forgiveness statements, she began to see that her loving was never the problem. She just grew up in an environment that didn't see her love or value it. She grew up in a home that had distorted beliefs about what love was, but Estelle's love was never the problem.

It dawned on Estelle that these beliefs that she created early on in her life also influenced her decision to marry a man who berated her, called her names, and never respected her. Estelle had truly believed that abuse was love. And so, she had found a man who would abuse her. Thankfully, something inside of Estelle knew that abuse wasn't right, and it was this part that got her out of her marriage. It was also this part of her that guided Estelle onto a path of healing.

After our work together, Estelle reported feeling happier, lighter, and more at peace. Everything changed for her.

She began dating a man who treated her with kindness and respect. Her anxiety lessened, and she began to trust her life.

Essentially, we updated Estelle. We had to remind the young traumatized parts of Estelle that she was no longer in an unsafe environment. We had to remind her that Estelle was now a 45-year-old woman who was competent and able to protect herself and create the boundaries she needed to feel safe. She was no longer six years old and subject to the abuse of her caregivers. Estelle was now her own caregiver and could treat herself with love, respect, and forgiveness.

As she continued to learn that she was safe and competent, Estelle's life blossomed. She eventually re-married and created a blended family that was supportive, nurturing, and loving. For the first time in her life, Estelle said she felt happy. She uncovered her own loving and healed her false beliefs and created happiness for herself. As she felt safe in her own loving, Estelle attracted a man who could really love her in a safe and kind way. She wound up creating a beautiful and loving family and felt true joy in her everyday life.

Pure Loving Energy
When you use this self-forgiveness process, you begin to replace false beliefs with loving. The false belief in your body or energy field dissolves. And loving rushes in to fill the empty spot. This is how we begin to love ourselves. The falsehoods, the untrue stories, and the dysfunctional beliefs are transmuted to pure loving. You will begin to feel

like yourself, possibly for the first time. Because the truth of who you are is this loving. The false beliefs covered up the loving that has wanted to rush through you from the moment of your birth. When we forgive ourselves, we come *home.*

If at any point you have trouble with this process, you can find a Noetic Field Therapist to help you. I've included a list of resources in the back of the book.

A Lifelong Process

Turning to the love within is something you can return to again and again throughout your life. It isn't as if we complete these exercises, clear these beliefs, and are healed always and forever. You will tap into your loving, reclaim lost parts of your energy, and feel tremendously better. However, life will continue presenting you with challenges. And every challenge is an opportunity to come into greater loving of yourself. Know that every difficulty is here to show you the path back home. And the path back home is to love yourself, accept yourself, and treat yourself kindly no matter what happens to you. To love yourself is to honor your needs, wants, and experiences. It is to offer loving to those parts of you that you abandoned or rejected to be normal, fit in, or make others happy. It is to offer loving to those parts of you that went into hiding when they felt that life was somehow unsafe.

This is what healing is. It isn't about fixing yourself so you can be perfect. It isn't about eliminating your imperfections, or abandoning the parts of yourself that you don't like. Quite the opposite. Healing is about bringing loving into those very imperfections and places inside of you that you've rejected in some way. You don't have to get rid of any part of yourself; you only have to extend loving, grace, and forgiveness to those parts. They just want YOU. Sometimes they think they want love from other people, but deep down, their singular yearning is to come back into harmony and loving with you. The parts of you that you've cut off, judged, or abandoned have never done anything wrong. They only need to be loved and brought back into the fold of all that you really are.

When you clear a belief, you heal it for the generations that come after you. When you heal a belief, you heal it for your children. You also offer the potential of healing to everyone you ever encounter. If your energy field changes, those who come into contact with you have the opportunity to change theirs as well. Very few might take it, and that's okay. But how great is it to know that as you heal yourself, you offer healing to those who come after you and to those all around you? It is like the icing on the cake. There are people who say doing self-work or healing is a selfish endeavor. Nope, quite the opposite. Through doing our own work, through examining our own dysfunctional beliefs, we heal not only ourselves but also the world around us. It is incredibly self-loving and also enables us to authentically love and embrace others and offer them the gift of finding their own healing.

Chapter 10
You Are Lovable—Even if You Don't Believe It

Dear One,

I see you
I see your tender heart
I see the wisdom in your Soul
I see how more than anything, you want to reach out and love
That tender heart of yours is gorgeous
It still beats, ruby red, with loving
I can feel it wanting love
You are loved
So deeply and truly
You are loved by your own Soul
You are loved by the Universe
You are loved by me
And you are loved by you

In my years of practice, I have found that nearly every belief can be traced back to one belief: *I am not worthy of love.* This seems to be the core belief we all adopt when we are born. It is the belief we try to heal when seeking approval and love from family, friends, co-workers, bosses, romantic partners, God, or anyone else we believe we need love from in order to be whole. When we aren't in touch with our own inherent worthiness that is based on the simple fact that we are divine beings, we try to search outside of ourselves to find a sense of worth. We think that if only we receive enough love from our spouse, or boss, or the family member who has ignored us for years, we will feel whole. We think that if we are skinny enough, or mild-mannered enough, or successful enough, or the perfect mother, that only then will we be worthy.

If we haven't tapped into our inherent worth, we will try to find worth by getting the outside world to approve of us, admire us, and love us. And none of this is bad; it all eventually leads us back to discovering our worth inside. Because the outside world is set up to disappoint you. It is set up so you will encounter the romantic partner who can't see the real you, or the boss who doesn't recognize what an incredible employee you are, or the family member who can't seem to accept you. This is perfection because it forces you to find the only sense of worth that is actually based on truth.

It is set up so that you have to uncover the love and worthiness inside of yourself.

This is the type of worth that cannot be taken away or removed. It is the truth of who you really are. You are not here to base your worth on any other person, organization, or job. You are here to find the worth that has already existed inside of you from the moment of your creation. You were born worthy. You were created worthy.

And the best part? When you know yourself as worthy, you bring all of the love and abundance to yourself you've been seeking. The more we know our worth, the better our relationships become and the more we open to receiving the abundance of the Universe. Worth is directly tied to the amount of love and abundance in your life. If you don't feel worthy of love or abundance, you will subconsciously keep it at arm's length. As you accept your inherent worthiness, you attract in partners, friends, and opportunities that truly nourish you.

Knowing that you are worthy, just as you are, is the key to fulfilling your dreams. Loving yourself now, just as you are, tells yourself that you are worthy. By forgiving and loving yourself, you treat yourself the way you want others to treat you.

You Don't Have to Love Yourself to Be Lovable
Even if you don't know or feel your worthiness, you are still worthy. Even if you don't know or feel your lovability, you are still lovable. There is nothing you can do to make yourself unlovable and unworthy of love. It is inherent in your *beingness*. You can't separate your cells from your

body. They are you. In the same way, loving and worthiness are you. They are as embedded in you as your very cells. You can't kick them out, even if you try. You are a divinely inspired being of light. Even when you don't feel like that divinely inspired being of light, you still are. There is nothing you ever did, and there is nothing you can ever do, to change or ruin that. The truth of the Universe is that no matter who you are, what you believe about yourself, or what others have said, you are a divine being of light. Even when you feel like the scum of the earth, behind it all, you are glorious love. Glorious light.

You are worthy. And you don't need to feel it or completely know it yet. If you don't yet believe you are worthy, you still are. You are worthy even when you don't believe you are. When we do this forgiveness work, we update you. We update the parts of you that still don't believe they are worthy. They always were, but now you get to educate them so that they *know* it. You get to bring them on board and let them know the truth of who and what they are — they were always lovable and will be always and forever.

You are worthy even if you don't fit with what society considers normal. You are worthy even if you've experienced abuse or trauma. You are worthy even if you are overweight or have a different color of skin than everyone around you, or make less money than your peers. You are worthy even if you are sick. You are worthy even if someone has dumped you. You are worthy even if you've

164

been abandoned and betrayed by parents, or friends, or lovers. You are worthy even if you are tall, short, and everything in between. You are worthy even if you've been told you are too skinny, or too flat-chested, or too anything.

You are worthy even if you have done something you weren't proud of. You are worthy even if you made a mistake. You are worthy even if you were addicted or cheated on your spouse. You are worthy even if you caused harm to another, either intentionally or unintentionally. We are always doing the best we can with what we have. The version of you who caused harm didn't know there was another option, or didn't have the strength to access a healthier option. Can you forgive yourself for judging yourself for not choosing a different path? Can you forgive yourself for judging yourself for not knowing how to do things differently? Can you forgive yourself for judging yourself for believing you are shameful and unworthy because of a dysfunctional response to a situation? You are deserving of forgiveness.

As we forgive ourselves, we actually empower ourselves to make healthier decisions in the future. If we remain in guilt and shame, we are actually more likely to perpetuate dysfunction. When we offer ourselves compassion and love, we heal, and are therefore more inclined to make better decisions in the future.

Nothing anyone can ever say or do will make you unworthy. It isn't possible. You simply get confused and forget your worth. When difficulties arise, you may think that those events are happening because some part of you isn't good enough, or strong enough, or beautiful enough, or safe enough. And so, you begin to hide yourself behind masks and protection. And that's okay. Your job now is to let yourself know that you are safe. You are a being with more experience, wisdom, and knowledge, and you can take care of yourself no matter what life brings. You can give yourself the space and freedom to allow yourself to be the real you.

All of the false beliefs you picked up along the way have been a means of helping you move into a place of self-discovery. You've been set up to see who you aren't, so you can move on and find who you *are*. Life has shown you the darkness and made it feel so awful that you had to go in search of the light. The light is who you really are. Even if you don't believe it, it is.

What Does Loving Yourself Look Like?
We've talked about undoing false beliefs so that you can unleash the loving that got tangled up in your heart. This is a necessary and profound way to begin to love yourself. And yet, it is also only part of how we learn to love ourselves.

Uncovering and clearing false beliefs starts to open up a whole new way of connecting with yourself. Through this process, we begin to develop a relationship with our self that becomes our most treasured relationship. We become our own beloved. And in doing so, we invite levels of loving that are unprecedented. We feel loving in our own bodies and hearts that warm us and fills us. We become warmed up from the inside by our own love. And the bonus is that once we learn to love ourselves, we attract people who can see and love the real us.

So, as we clear out false beliefs, we uncover a new relationship with our true beloved: our Self. This new relationship is important to nurture. It is the source of true happiness, joy, and fulfillment. This relationship with our Self is a prerequisite to a successful partnership or romantic relationship. When we know and love ourselves, we can know and love another.

Spend Time Connecting to Your Soul

Some of my favorite times are when I am alone, connecting to myself and loving the precious moments I get to have with my own Soul. From the age of 18, I've been taking myself on retreats to our family cabin in Colorado. When I am there, no one is around for at least a half mile, and it is quiet, sometimes lonely, but also deeply silent and connective in a way I can't fully put into words. On my brief, two-day retreats, I like to play music, cook myself a delicious dinner, dance around the cabin, and simply enjoy myself. I go for walks with my dog, I meditate, and I paint. I allow myself to be guided by whatever my heart desires. Some days that means spending an entire day watching movies on the couch. Other days that includes writing, or snow-shoeing, or taking a hot bath. These times of sacred silence and retreat are precious.

Truthfully, there are times when being alone and connecting to my Soul is more fulfilling than any experience with my friends, family, or partner. Our connection with our Self can be the most wonderful, nurturing, and satisfying experience there is. So many of us run from being alone, from connecting to our own selves. But when we do, there are incredible gifts waiting for us there. When you sit through the loneliness, the idleness, the crazy chatter of the mind and allow the heart to guide you into its next longing, happiness awaits. Joy is present.

I encourage you to begin to develop a relationship with your Self, if you have not already. It is the only relationship that is guaranteed to never end. You will not be abandoned; you will not be heartbroken. When you become your own best friend, you are with yourself always.

This is the path of self-love and the path of true happiness and joy.

Conclusion

Dear Sweet Soul, you are one of the brave ones. You are one of the few who is willing to look into that heart of yours to see what is there. It takes courage to look within, at the soft places, the hurt places, and the places inside of you that don't believe they are worthy. Not many choose this journey. You are a warrior of the heart, ready to examine the demons of shame and fear that have taken up residence inside of you and that threaten you with messages that you aren't enough.

You *are* enough. You are more than enough. You are glorious.

I know it isn't easy. I know the journey of healing — the journey of excavating your real self from the rubble of false beliefs, criticisms, and intentional and accidental heart aches and breaks and traumas you've picked up along the way — is tough work. This work that you are about to do, while magical and full of sweet release, takes a certain amount of bravery. You are that brave one. You are a kickass warrior of the heart, willing to move away the rubble and debris to find

the shiny treasure of your own True Self. And the jewels
you find within yourself will make this entire journey worth
it. Joy, freedom, and love are the hidden treasures inside
of you that are about to be released. You can finally start
to *live*.

True healing occurs when we offer ourselves the loving
we so desperately want from others. It takes place when we
stop needing love outside of ourselves to feel whole, and
instead offer the very love we are craving to ourselves, from
ourselves. It happens when we stop trying to change other
people and their treatment of us, and instead turn inside and
offer tenderness to the parts of us that want others to treat us
with total love and appreciation. It happens when we forgive
the false beliefs that we adopted and replace those beliefs
with loving.

Your worthiness and loving can never be taken away.
The absolutely amazing news is that when you find a home
within yourself, when you find the loving and worthiness
within, it can't be removed. When that loving or worthiness
depends on people in your life and their treatment of you,
you're in a bit of trouble. If they withdraw their loving and
attention, you lose your sense of loving and worthiness.
When it is based on your own loving of yourself, you
always have it. What other people do or don't do won't
matter as much. You'll always have your home of loving to
return to when you need it. And when people make choices
that violate you, you'll be more willing to protect your inner
space of loving. You'll safeguard it and keep it, because it

will be what sustains you. You will begin to cherish your own self and protect that sacred sweetness that lives inside of you. Other people and their love won't be what sustains you and keeps you going. You'll take the pressure off them to love you and to fill your holes with their love. You'll fill your own heart holes with loving. Ironically, they are then free to love even more, in a way that is free of dependency.

When you make your home-base your own loving, you give permission for people to be in their loving. And two people who have found the loving inside, and have made their own loving their home, can come together to play in ways that are light, free, and spontaneous.

Happiness, joy, and play are your destiny. They start with forgiveness and love.

Beloved, gorgeous Being, may loving, light, and forgiveness find you and hold you close.

Example False Beliefs

I've included a list of example false beliefs that I've seen come up repeatedly when working with clients. Some of these beliefs might resonate with you; in which case, do the forgiveness statement process with them from Chapter 9. Otherwise, use these beliefs to stir up any other beliefs that you sense you may have picked up along the way.

Beliefs about Love:
The people I love leave me.
Love will always abandon me.
I'm unworthy of being cared about.
The world is unsafe and I must always protect myself.
There is danger lurking around every corner.
I'm not special enough to be loved.
I'm not pretty enough to be loved.
I'm not good enough to be loved.
There is something very wrong with me.
I'm unlovable.
Loving others is painful and dangerous.

It is unsafe to love.

My love pushes people away.

I have to be alone in life to be safe.

Loving another makes me dependent on them.

Beliefs about Gender:[*]

Feminine:

I have to be perfect to be loved.

Women who are worthy of love are thin, tall, etc.

Women who are worthy of love are always nice and gentle.

A woman's value is in her appearance.

I have to be the perfect mother.

Being the perfect mother means _____.

I'm shameful because I'm a woman.

I can't be desired and powerful at the same time.

I should always have less and be less than men.

To be safe, I need to hide my truest self.

It is unsafe for me to have power.

Power is dominance.

My emotions make me weak.

Emotions are useless.

---

[*] This does not necessarily correlate to what sex you are, as each of us has a combination of masculine and feminine inside.

Masculine:

Men who are worthy of love are strong.

Men who are worthy of love don't show their emotions.

Men are worthy based on their ability to provide for a family.

Being vulnerable will kill me.

I'm unlovable if I fail.

I'm unworthy if I fail.

It is shameful to be vulnerable.

I have to be accepted by women before I can be loved.

I need women to accept me before I am worthy.

I have to dominate to be a real man.

I have to shut myself down in order to be strong.

Strength means being invincible.

Beliefs about Success:

Success is having a job, getting married, and raising 2.5 children.

Success means looking perfect.

Success is about owning a home.

I am worthy because of what I do.

I am worthy because of my education.

It is unsafe to be successful.

It is unsafe to have all that I want in life.

I am what I do professionally.

The amount of money I make determines my worth.

I have to compete and win in order to be safe.

Power makes me safe.

Beliefs about Money:
I can't make money without the help of a man.
I'm unworthy of receiving.
I'm only worthy because of how much I give.
If I make money, I have to give it all to a man.
People from my kind of background don't have money.
In order to be spiritual, I have to be poor.
Poverty is sacred.
Only the poor get into heaven.
Money is evil.
People who have money are greedy, bad, and selfish.
If people are envious or jealous of me, I've done something bad or wrong.
If I have money, I will take away from or hurt people who don't.

Beliefs about Relationships:
I have to be loyal to people who hurt me in order to be loved.
People who hurt me do it because they love me.
I'm unworthy of a great romantic relationship.
I have to give myself away to be in a relationship.
I have to sacrifice myself for the relationship.
I have to give up my needs to my partner in order to be loved.
My value in my relationship comes from how much I give.
I can only be desired for how much I give.

I have to be perfect before I can be loved and accepted.

My partner needs me to be perfect.

I cannot pursue my spirituality and have a relationship at the same time.

Love is abuse.

Beliefs about Happiness:

I can't be happy until my family is happy.

I can't be happy until my partner is happy.

I can't be happy until my children are happy.

I can't be happy until the world is at peace.

I can't be happy until everyone is happy.

I can't be happy until_____.

I can't have what I want in life.

I'm a horrible person who doesn't deserve to have what I want.

Beliefs about Spirituality:

God wants me to suffer.

I have to sacrifice myself to make God happy.

I have to sacrifice myself to get to heaven.

My desires don't matter to God.

I don't deserve to return to God.

God needs me to be perfect.

I have to give myself away to get to God.

I deserve to be punished.

<u>Beliefs about Our Bodies</u>:

I'm bad if I am overweight.

I have to be thin before I can be worthy.

My weight is who I really am.

I cannot be happy until I am _____ (skinny, buff, etc.).

Because of the way my body is, I have to hide from people.

If I overeat or binge, I am worthless.

My body is shameful.

Sex is a sin.

Enjoying my body means I will be punished.

Enjoying food makes me a bad person.

<u>Beliefs about Life</u>:

Bad things are always waiting around the corner.

If I enjoy my life, something bad will happen.

Life is meant to be suffered through.

Resources

To find additional information, resources, articles, and ways to work with me, please visit my website:
www.charmaynekilcup.com

To find additional healers who specialize in the techniques described in this book visit:
http://www.noeticbalancing.com

To find a therapist visit:
www.psychologytoday.com

To find the degree program mentioned, visit:
www.swc.edu

If you are interested in becoming a practitioner of this work, visit:
www.instituteofspiritualcoaching.com

www.livinginthepresence.net

Acknowledgments

Thank you to my clients, for your unwavering courage to do this work. I'm so deeply honored to be part of your journey and to witness your incredible souls.

Thank you to Robert Waterman and Karey Thorne, for your guidance, wisdom, loving, and service. You both have transformed my life in ways that are indescribable in words. I am so grateful for your presence on this planet.

Thank you to my editor, Lara Asher, who took a mess of words and created a book out of them. Without you to hold my hand, I would never have felt comfortable enough to release this into the world.

Thank you to Dr. Kaelyn Langer-Mendonca, for your feedback and love.

Thank you to my biological and spiritual families: Walter, Mom, Dad, Grandpa, Cam, Cailyn, Sarah, Laurie, Jessica, Christen, and Ken. Thank you for being my tribe and supporting me in taking the path less chosen.

About the Author

Charmayne Kilcup, PhD, is a Heart & Soul Coach, who specializes in helping people recover from heartache, emotional trauma, and spiritual crises. She has firsthand experience overcoming difficult situations — she has struggled with eating disorders, multiple heart breaks, chronic fatigue, health scares, and a spiritual awakening that knocked her on her ass and turned her world upside down. She had to find ways of understanding her life and her path and transforming her pain into joy — and she has.

After her own awakening, Charmayne studied with some incredible teachers and learned some absolutely life-changing techniques for healing . . . and living. Now she feels a deep sense of loving that courses through her veins, a loving that goes beyond her relationships and passions. It is a loving that lives inside of her and never dies. Her passion is to use what she's learned to help others work through their own heartaches, heartbreaks, and spiritual crises and come back into alignment with themselves.

Charmayne received her MA in Counseling from Southwestern College, in Santa Fe, New Mexico, and her PhD from Sofia University, in Palo Alto, California. She is also trained in Noetic Field Therapy®, ThetaHealing®, and Reconnective Healing. Charmayne has served as adjunct faculty at Sofia University and Southwestern College. She has a private practice and works with people both in-person and long distance.

She lives in Santa Fe, New Mexico, with her husband, Walter, and their two rescue dogs, Lula and Ruby. You can visit her website at www.charmaynekilcup.com.

Made in the USA
Middletown, DE
21 November 2023

43226785R00137